CW01501904

The DANGER of UXB's

TRUE STORIES OF BOMB DISPOSAL
HEROISM IN WORLD WAR II

CONTRIBUTED BY THOSE WHO WERE THERE

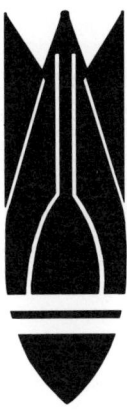

Lt Col Eric Wakeling (Ret'd)

A B D PUBLISHING PUBLICATION

First published in 1996 by
B D Publishing
6 Wendover Road, BOURNE END. Bucks. SL8 5NT

British Library Cataloguing Publication Data. A catalogue record of this book is available from the British Library.

Wakeling, Eric E.
The DANGER of UXB's: Collected stories of Bomb Disposal heroism in World War II

ISBN 0 9525799 2 8

Typeset by B D Publishing, Bourne End. Bucks.
Monochromes by Gem Offset Printers, High Wycombe. Bucks.
Printed by Rexam Digital Imaging Ltd, Reading. Berks.

By the same author

The Lonely War

A Photographic Story of Bomb Disposal

To Nicky

Without whose continued patience and understanding no books would have been written, let alone a third !

AUTHORS NOTE

At the outbreak of World War II, the British Army had just one Chemical 'Defence' Company. RE.

Because of the memories of the 1914/18 war, when gas was used extensively towards the end, the Government put in a crash programme to produce a large number of Chemical 'Warfare' Companies.

A Training Battalion was established not far from Porton Down, at the time the centre for Chemical Warfare, at Winterbourne Dauntsey. The first three Companies raised and trained (?) were posted to France on 1st January 1940.

By the May, three other Training Battalions were formed at Barton Stacey, near Andover. All were designed to form and train the Companies.

Each Company had a Headquarters and three Sections. In the way of transport, each Section had a P.U. (Pickup truck) Thirteen 15 cwt and three 30 cwt trucks. All issued 'Brand new'.

They were never used in the original role for which they were trained and 'reroled' about two years later.

In contrast, in May of that year, as will be seen in the following pages, the powers that be decided there was a need for some Bomb Disposal units. The original ones consisted of a L/Cpl and a couple of men. In the June, larger units were formed, with an officer in charge, usually a newly commissioned 2/Lieut, straight from OCTU, with a Sgt and 14 men.

Originally, they were not issued with transport ! Later they received 'impressed' vehicles, such as coal lorries, cattle trucks, furniture vans, etc.

There was no Training Battalion formed. The men went out with little or no training. In fact, the first Army Bomb Disposal Training School did not open its doors until 22nd July 1941.

Most of the officers and men, who were not killed, continued in Bomb Disposal until the end of the war. They faced possible death almost every day of the war and yet were not given any recognition for their bravery and devotion to duty.

This book is about those men, by those men. All the stories in this book are true, contributed by the men themselves and the citations for their bravery.

At its peak, more than 20,000 Royal Engineers were engaged in Bomb Disposal. Between them they were awarded just thirteen George Crosses and 105 George Medals. Many more should have been awarded.

FOREWORD

by

Major General C N Thompson CB BA FRICS MIMgt

All those who served in Bomb Disposal in the Second World War, those who have served since and those who are still serving in this field, will be grateful to Eric Wakeling for his collection of true stories of Wartime Bomb Disposal. There were many unsung heroes who, day in and day out, carried out the lonely war against the UXB. As Eric commented in his first book, The Lonely War, the disposal of the UXB went on 365 days a year - the next bomb was always ready and waiting.

Unlike Eric Wakeling, who admits to having volunteered, the experience of most people in Bomb Disposal is that they were 'volunteered' through the mysteries of the posting system. They came from a diversity of backgrounds with a mixture of skills, got on with the job in hand and in doing so showed outstanding dedication and no small measure of courage over long periods of time - and with very little respite from the ever present danger that is inherent in every UXB.

Many acts of heroism in Bomb Disposal have been recorded and the award of the George Cross, the George Medal and other awards for gallantry to so many in Bomb Disposal is some small measure of their achievements and the achievements of all who served in Bomb Disposal during the War. Most of these are recorded in this volume and having tapped a rich vein of human endeavour let us hope that Eric will carry on his highly commendable work which helps to strengthen the bonds that exist between all those who had the privilege to serve in this field.

25th July 1996

ILLUSTRATIONS.

CONTENTS

Introduction

The contents of this book are, mainly, verbatim stories, as told by wartime Bomb Disposal Officers, Sgts and other ranks, about their various 'jobs', as bomb incidents were referred to. In addition, the citations of all the 13 George Crosses and most of the 105 George Medals awarded for heroism and bravery during the 1939/45 war are included. A complete list of those so awarded is shown in the Appendices.

The text is supported by various photographs which were taken at the time. We are fortunate in that in spite of the shortage of films at the time and a 'Restriction' that photographs should not be taken, the more entrepreneurial of us managed to record some of our efforts.

Many of these photos have only just come to light as a result of an appeal to the members of the 'Retired Bomb Disposal Officers Club'. Yes, some of us did retire. We were not all blown up, although there are many members who have suffered injuries, such as blindness and the loss of limbs.

Earlier books have paid tribute to the work of Bomb Disposal Officers during the last war. Many of whom were awarded the George Cross, the George Medal, the MBE and later, the Queen's Gallantry Medal, even one Distinguished Service Cross, which is a Naval Medal and was awarded for gallantry in the Falklands War.

For some inexplicable reason, whilst there was no recognition, in the form of a medal for our wartime exploits, be it officer or other rank, the 'Powers that be' decided to have a medal struck and awarded to those who were engaged in Bomb Disposal or Minefield Clearance from V.E. day to the end of 1949.There was a requirement of 180 days working on either, or both, operations. Very few were issued and it is not a medal which can be quoted after a persons name, such as the George Cross. It is called the 'General Service Medal', with Bomb Disposal and Minefield clasp ! In spite of it's plebeian title, each medal, which is engraved with name of the person to whom it was awarded, is now worth over £400.

This book, which recognises the valour of the officers and men who were, literally, *On Active Service for five years, even though they didn't leave the U.K.*

All the stories in this book are true, having been told by those who were actually there at the time and participated to the full. It will be seen that for much of the time everything was dealt with with some sort of levity. It was really the only way with which one could deal with the constant pressures and stay sane. 'Counselling' was unheard of in those days. To us, as it was to every other chap, who was serving his Country - A JOB TO BE DONE - Be it in the desert, or Burma, on a ship, either Royal Navy or Merchant Service, or in the air, fighting or bombing. Or, for that matter, the Fire Service or Civil Defence in our towns which were bombed almost every night.

The 1939/45 war was a TOTAL war. We were all involved. I merely make the point that, to a great extent, *our lives were in our own hands.* Whether we lived or died depended upon our ability to work inches away from a bomb, which could blow us to eternity. To identify the fuze or fuzes and have the knowledge and expertise to render it, or them, safe. Thus preventing an explosion which would have destroyed yet more houses or, more importantly at the time, a factory which was producing guns, or tanks, or aircraft, or whatever was needed for the war effort.

Talk to any wartime Bomb Disposal Officer, who spent the war in the U.K. and he will tell you what a 'Good War' he had ! At least we all slept in a bed every night - be it our own or someone else's ! Which is more than can be said for those who were in North Africa, the Middle East, Burma and France. Although I must record that Bomb Disposal Companies were in Malta, North Africa, Italy, the Middle East, India, the Far East and later went to France, Belgium, Holland and Germany. Some of the stories of their experiences are included.

The length of the chapters in this book vary considerably, as it contains the collected stories of those who served at the time. Each chapter, therefore, depended upon what was received from those officers and men who were able to put their memories on paper.

The same applies to photographs. In the early days, no one thought of recording their activities - We just didn't have time to even THINK about photos and the 'professional' newspaper photographers didn't want to get TOO close - It was only, much later, that the cameras came out to record our activities. Hence there are more records of the later wars years.

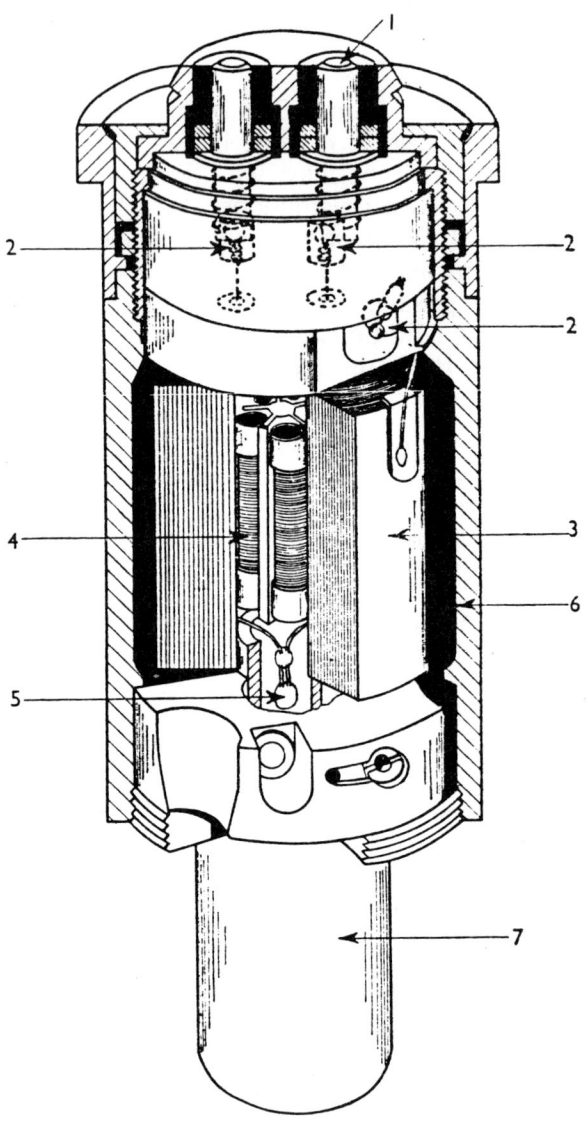

Sectional view of a No (15) fuze.

1. Plungers
2. Impact switches
3. Condensers
4. Resistances

5. Firing Bridge
6. Pitch filling
7. Gaine

Chapter One

PRE WAR AND OUR FORMATION.

The Spanish civil war was the proving ground for Germany, Italy and Russia. Particularly in the sphere of aerial warfare. Not only did they use their planes but also their bombs and, in the case of Germany, their newly designed electrical fuzes.

By their support of General Franco, the Germans and Italians received many reports on the effect and potential of their bombs and fuzing systems, all of which came through with such good results that further research and development were ordered.

It has always amazed the author that neither British Intelligence nor those responsible for our Civil Defence, ever consulted the vast amount of information which was currently available to all, from the 'Newsreels' we saw in the cinema every day. Some of it was actually in the Patents office. It was later discovered that the German manufacturer of the fuzes had lodged details of them with that august body, in about 1935.

The raids on major towns and cities in Spain had shown the necessity of an Air Raid Precautions organisation. After 'Munich' panic measures were taken. Shelters, anti-gas precautions, emergency centres for feeding, medical and police were all put into effect. But no office within the Government thought about the unexploded bomb.

At the outbreak of war, the subject of Bomb Disposal was, to say the least, a very low priority. That is if anyone was giving it any attention at all. Firstly, it was considered to be the responsibility of the Home Office. They planned that any bombs found would be collected by the ARP Wardens and taken to convenient dumps, where they would later be blown up by the Army. Why the Royal Air Force was never consulted will remain a mystery. THEY, at least, must have been aware of what happened to bombs when they were dropped and failed to explode. They had many unexploded bombs in the ground on their bombing ranges !

Much later, information from Poland brought details of 'long delay' electrical fuzes.

The Research and Experiments Branch of the Ministry of Home Security proposed, amongst others, to train and equip a special ARP force, for dealing with UXB's. Such proposals were submitted to 'Higher Authority' but nothing was done to implement them. Instead, the Army was asked to provide Bomb Disposal teams, until such time as the ARP squads could be trained.

The Army agreed and teams of three men - An NCO and two sappers - were formed. Their job was to dig down to the bomb and explode it *in situ*. It was also included in their 'Job Specification' that they should train the ARP personnel. Unfortunately, for the Royal Engineers, the ARP personnel failed to appear.

The very first raid on the U.K. is reported as being on 16th October. German bombers tried to demolish the Forth bridge. Four German aircraft were shot down. However, it was not until just before Christmas when a seaplane base in the Shetlands was bombed and we experienced our first unexploded bombs. Four 5Økg bombs from the raid failed to explode. They penetrated the ground to between six and ten feet. It would have been deeper, but for the rocky ground. They were dug up and the fuzes were despatched to the Research Dept at Woolwich for examination. The 'boffins' took them apart and worked out a method of immunising the (15) fuze, for that was their number. The equipment was designed and produced.

Early in 1940, we experienced a few more raids, some more in Scotland and others along the East coast of the country. They began to concentrate the minds of the 'Powers that be'. Some of the bombs had not gone off and the question began to manifest itself to the extent where it could not be ignored. How would we cope if there were a large number of unexploded bombs, which prevented, for example, the rail movement of troops and ammunition, and production in factories where tanks, ammunition, ships etc, were being manufactured.

It was, at last, realised that a properly organised force, under military discipline, was needed and in February 1940, it was agreed that the War Office would take over the responsibility of dealing with all unexploded bombs in the U.K. It was also agreed that the Navy and RAF, would have the responsibility for dealing with any bombs which fell on their stations. The Navy were also given the responsibility for any missile which came to rest below the normal High water Mark of both a tidal river and coast. The Ministry of Supply was given the responsibility of providing all Services with whatever equipment they needed to immunise enemy missiles.

Naturally, the Army responsibility fell to the Royal Engineers. Why not ? They had, in the first World War, brought in the first tanks, the first signals communications and had had their own torpedoes, for the defence of London and the Medway Towns. Not forgetting that the Royal Flying Corps was formed from officers of the Royal Engineers and their ground staff.

The first step was to form 'Ad Hoc' sections, of an officer and a few men, who had to deal with everything thrown at them; but it was soon realised that they were not coping and that more men were required, with a supporting organisation. Thus they were 'absorbed' within the new 25 Bomb Disposal Sections which were authorised with a Lieutenant, a Sgt and fourteen men, most of which were not operational until much later in the year. When one looks at the 'Order of Battle' of B D Companies since 1942, it is obvious, from the section numbers, who were the 'early birds' ! It will be seen that some of the companies, formed later, had no experienced men. All their sections were new, with the officer coming straight from OCTU (Officer Cadet Training Unit) and the men, probably straight from a holding or training Depot.

The early sections, of an officer and a few men, suffered from the lack of equipment - and knowledge. They had hammers and chisels, a few digging tools, a small quantity of explosives. Often, they didn't even have any transport and had to WALK to their 'Bomb job'. In addition, there was no 'Chain of Command'. They were independent, found a home with a unit in the area for 'Rations and Accommodation' - A favourite expression in those days.

From the bombs recovered at the Shetlands it was evident that with larger bombs, it would be impossible to blow them up where they were found and a method had to be found to immunise the fuze and remove it, without incurring any danger to the officer carrying out the removal, so that the bomb could be rendered safe and removed to a site where it could be blown up without causing any damage.

This would be of particular importance where bombs were found in factories or stores. The first piece of equipment was the 'Crabtree Two pin' Discharger. The Boffins had discovered that if the two plungers in the boss of the fuze were depressed, the electrical charge would soon be earthed and the fuze rendered inert. A few months after this piece of equipment had been issued, it was discovered that the Germans had introduced a (25) fuze into their armoury. It was very similar to the (15). BUT, if the plungers were depressed, the bomb would explode. The 'Crabtree Discharger' was 'OUT'. As soon as a No (25) had been recovered, It was sent to the Research Dept,

Woolwich, who rapidly designed a new piece of equipment, called the 'B D Discharger'. This piece of equipment was designed to insinuate a liquid, past the plungers, without depressing them, which would short out the condensers in the fuze. It worked every time. Unfortunately, a large number of lives were lost before it was discovered that by pressing the plungers of a (25) the bomb exploded. So, even before the 'Deluge' commenced, when the Germans transferred their attention from RAF airfields to London and other cities, our losses were already much too high.

However, before this had been invented, came the organisation of R E Bomb Disposal, but this was not an easy time. It was not until June 1940, that 25 B D Companies were authorised. But it takes time to form that number of Companies; not only are officers and men required, there is also equipment, transport, accommodation, etc. But by then, many acts of bravery had been carried out. George Crosses and George Medals had been awarded to the many who, not knowing what they were doing, disarmed many bombs, under horrendous conditions.

The life expectancy of a B D Officer was, at the most, sixteen weeks. Many did not survive even that period.

At the War Office, the Inspector of Fortifications (Who was probably a Gunner) was given the additional responsibility of 'Director of Bomb Disposal', hence IF & DBD. This only lasted a few months, when a separate War Office Department was formed:- The Directorate of Bomb Disposal. Our original 'Boss', Major General Taylor, was very concerned at the early losses of officers. Subsequently, he moved on and we had Brigadier Bateman, who was also a very humane man, so interested in the welfare of his officers and men. He visited us constantly. He was followed by a more aptly named Brigadier, who was his equal, but had the unfortunate name of De'ath, which was not a good omen for anyone in our job.

After Dunkirk, the RAF airfields were being hammered and it was partly due to Hitler changing his mind that we won the 'Battle of Britain'. (With no disrespect to the valiant pilots of Fighter Command.) It was a 'war of attrition' which we nearly lost and could well have done, if Hitler had continued to send his fighters and bombers to blast the RAF, not only out of the skies, but also out of their airfields. In the September he changed the Luftwaffe targets to towns and cities, of which London was the main target.

It was very fortunate for this country that it had been realised we were inadequately prepared for heavy bombing raids even though the formation of B D Companies had been authorised. Whilst we might not have been at the pitch of our efficiency, or even ready by September 1940, when the 'Blitz' on London really started, at least we were partially ready - and we learnt extremely fast - we had to !

The majority of B D Subalterns were posted straight from OCTU, (Officer Cadet Training Unit) regardless of their qualifications. In the event, history tells us that they were given an RE commission because of their qualifications and they were mostly architects ! - those who had hoped to design buildings, rather than prevent their destruction.

All ranks, in Bomb Disposal were advised that, after a six month tour of duty, they could opt to transfer to another branch of the Corps. It was made because it was thought that after such a period, some might be suffering from nervous strain or exhaustion. (Counselling had never been heard of !) Very few, if any, took advantage of the option. In fact, quite a few officers actually 'Volunteered' for Bomb Disposal. (The author and several others mentioned doing just that !)

As already mentioned, for a few months, the only known German fuze was the (15), from the Shetland bombs. It was the RAF who gave us the training, which was mainly 'In principal'. British fuzes were entirely different from German. For example, British, American, French - in fact any other nation apart from Germany - used 'Nose' and 'Tail' fuzes, which were all mechanical, armed by a little propeller which spun round as the bomb travelled earthwards. The German fuzes were in the SIDE of the bomb and were armed 'electrically'. One advantage of this was that, whereas a 'nose' fuze was usually damaged beyond recognition in an unexploded British bomb, the 'side' fuze of a German bomb was usually recognisable.

One officer who went went on No 2 Course at RAF Melksham recorded in his diary that *My RAF Form 619 - Small notebook for use in schools - has extensive notes on Explosives, fillings, types of bombs, some sizes and weights of British Bombs, their markings and colour, but remarkably little about German Bombs.*

The course was supposed to last a week. On the first day we were lectured ad infinitum on RAF bombs and, in the Mess that evening, we wondered if or when we were to be told about German bombs.

On the second day we were told that the German fuzing system was based an electrical fuze and that there were two plungers in the head of the fuzes. It seemed that most of the information was from the Spanish civil war

In the afternoon the C.O. - A Wing Commander - addressed us, patted us on our respective backs, told us that we had all passed and handed us our equipment - A two pronged 'Crabtree' fuze discharger. He wishes us jolly good luck and said how delighted they would be if we could bring any German bombs and fuzes back to Melksham. He then said that as they couldn't tell us any more, we could all return to our units.

As we were to find out later in the war, the Germans were very methodical. Every number meant something. The common denominator was a (5). i.e. (15), (25), both of which were impact or short delay fuzes, as were (8)'s. a (38) was usually used in an armour piercing bomb when attacking ships. (9) were airburst fuzes, for releasing small incendiary or anti personnel bombs from big a container. (7) were delay fuzes, the (17) being the most prolific and any fuze number ending in '∅', was a booby trap, the No (5∅) being the most common, used in conjunction of the long delay (17), often with a ZUS 4∅ under the (17). This combination meant that we couldn't stop the ticking clock of a (17), because any movement would set off the (5∅) and we couldn't take the No (17) out of the bomb, because if we did, the ZUS 4∅ under it would explode the bomb - CATCH 22 !"

By then end of 194∅, we had but two pieces of equipment; The Crabtree 2 pin discharger and the fuze key, which enabled us to unscrew the locking ring holding the fuze in the bomb. - It replaced the 'Hammer and Chisel' !

By the end of 1941, we had a whole range of equipment. But as fast as the boffins produced a piece of equipment to counteract a new piece of German chicanery, the Germans managed to produce a new fuze. By the end of the war, many of the fuzes produced by the Germans were not designed to explode the bomb on impact, or shortly after, but to kill the British B D Officer when he tried to immunise it.

It was a war between 'Boffins' and the PBBDO (Poor Bloody B D Officer) was in the middle.

Chapter Two

IN THE BEGINNING

My wife and I were in the sitting room of the Married Quarters occupied by the Commanding Officer of 33 Engineer Regiment. (EOD) - (Explosive Ordnance Disposal) - Then, Lt Col Chris Sexton and his wife, Annie.

Also with us was Col B S T Archer GC OBE ERD ('Archie') and his wife Kit. Col Archer was, at that time, the President of the Victoria Cross and George Cross Association. In that capacity he had accompanied H M The Queen Mother for three days, during the V E Day celebrations in May 1995 and later over the VJ Day activities.

Naturally, talk had got round to wartime Bomb Disposal and I asked Archie how he got into it. He told us that he was in the T.A. before the war, in the Honourable Artillery Company. Even 'Other Ranks' in the 'HAC' were usually 'Something in the City!' Archie was an architect. Soon after the outbreak of war most, if not all, members of the HAC were recommended for a commission and were shipped off to various OCTUs. (Officer Cadet Training Unit). Because of his profession, Archie was sent to a Royal Engineer OCTU. After a short course he was commissioned and immediately posted to Bomb Disposal. (So much for architecture ! - Mind you, we did do our best to prevent it from being blown up !)

Kit (Who was then in her eighties !) started to tell us about Archie's first bomb. He corrected her by saying

"*That was not my first bomb*" and proceeded to tell us about the early days of June 1940.

He was posted to Cardiff, with a Sgt and half a dozen men with a few picks and shovels but very little else. - In those days, the Home Office still thought that a couple of men and a barrow could go round collecting unexploded bombs. In spite of the information that the Civil War in Spain could have provided.

They moved into some accommodation on arrival and settled down for the night. About 0300 hrs, Archie was woken by someone from the A R P and told that there was a bomb in the docks. He was taken by their car to the site, where he saw a hole in the ground.

Now, he had never seen a hole in the ground before. On his very short B D course at RAF Mamby, he saw a few bombs exhibited, all on the ground ! He tried to visualize the size of the bomb from the hole in the ground - probably a 500lb or 1000lb he thought.

He was taken back to their billet, where he assembled his men and they then *marched* (They had no transport !) to the docks.

BY THE TIME THEY GOT THERE, THE BOMB HAD EXPLODED !!!

As Archie said; "*Now, THAT was my FIRST bomb.*" Obviously, not the first he had to defuze, but certainly his introduction to the hazards of 1940 Bomb Disposal ! When the life expectancy of a B D Officer was a short one !

Unfortunately, Kit did not have time to tell us about Archie's first *real* bomb ! After, Archie had to admit that he couldn't remember his first bomb, which, knowing of his activities at that time, is not a surprise. Fortunately, some of those activities were recorded and he was awarded the George Cross. Not for just one 'job', but for several. Even then, it was almost a year later before his award was promulgated in the London Gazette. His citations reads;-

"Second Lieut Archer has been employed on Bomb Disposal work since June 1940, and has dealt with some two hundred bombs, in addition to incidents mentioned below. He provided the War Office with fuzes numbered (17), (25), (26), (38) and (50) fuzes plus a Zus 40 anti handling device for experiment, at a time when little was known about the nature of German fuzes.

On 15th July 1940 four 250 kg bombs were dropped in St Athan aerodrome, South Wales, two within ten yards of some vitally important assembly sheds. Lieut Archer immediately went to the scene and the first bomb was excavated. As it's fuze was expected to be a booby trap, it was loaded, with the fuze still in, on to a lorry. Lt Archer himself drove the lorry to a site some two miles away and the bomb was detonated. The other bombs were dealt with in the same way.

On the 17th August 1940 at Moulton, South Wales, a 250 kg bomb was excavated down to the fuze pocket, which contained a No (50) fuze. As this fuze was required for War Office experiments, an attempt was made to extract it by means of a cord and, when this failed Lieut Archer removed it by hand by means of a pickaxe head, although well aware that the fuze might be a booby trap..

On 27th August, at Port Talbot Docks, he was instrumental in recovering the first No (38) fuze for experimental purposes.

On 2nd September 1940, a vast fire was started in six oil storage tanks after a heavy raid on the National Oil Refineries at Skewen, near Swansea. There were unexploded bombs in and around the oil tank farm and Lieut Archer and his party went to work some eight hours after the raid. In spite of the fact that three bombs had exploded, he and his men remained working. One 250 kg bomb had fallen two feet from the side of an oil tank and when uncovered was found to contain a No (17) fuze, which was ticking. Lieut Archer was able to remove the filler cap, scrape away the explosive and remove the whole fuze pocket, which had sheared. As the fuze was required for experiment he removed it by hand from the exploder tube and found a Zus 40 anti handling device which had not functioned and this too he removed by hand. This was apparently the first Zus 40 to be successfully extricated.

In addition to the above incidents, Lieut Archer has on three occasions driven lorries containing bombs armed with No (17) fuzes in order to remove them from sites.

The Inspector of Fortifications and Director of Bomb Disposal stated; *The fact that Lieut Archer has enjoyed such remarkable immunity from death in no way detracts from his record of deliberate and sustained courage coupled with devotion to duty of the highest order".*

* * * * * * * * * * * *

Lieut Col R T Harris was awarded the George Cross, whilst still a civilian, when he was a Staff Officer of the Croydon ARP Engineer Service and a member of the Borough Engineers Dept.

Croydon was frequently and heavily bombed in 1940 with many bombs failing to explode. Mr Harris, as he was then, was the Liaison Officer between Croydon ARP and the RE Bomb Disposal Company at Kingston.

At the beginning of the raids he did little more than locate the bombs and leave the Sappers to recover them. Later, as the Bomb Disposal Company became more heavily engaged, it was only possible to send out small parties of junior ranks to deal with the incidents and Mr Harris often assumed unofficial charge of the disposal operations and disarmed highly sensitive bombs himself.

He was later commissioned in the Royal Engineers.

* * * * * * * * * * * *

Sgt Bill Edwards was posted to No 2 B D Company, whose H Q was in a T.A. Drill Hall, called Signals House, in Atkins Road, Balham. Obviously, the peace time home of a Royal Corps of Signals unit. He worked on B D operations in London until January 1941 when he was posted to No 18 B D Company, which went out to the Middle East.

He remembers walking along a road and coming across a double decker bus, which had passed him earlier, now nose down in a very large crater. He assisted the driver out of his cab who, fortunately, suffered only from a injured arm. The bomb had fallen earlier and exploded in the Underground, hence the rather large crater.

* * * * * * * * * * * *

This citation for a George Medal epitomises the bravery of those officers and men, who were in Bomb Disposal from the early days of May and June of 1940. The officer concerned commanded 10 B D Section of No 4 B D Company, based at Bury St Edmunds.

"Lieut Kenneth Dickinson has been engaged upon Bomb Disposal duties since June 1940. On 18th August an unexploded bomb fell within the confines of Shoeburyness Garrison. He immediately went to the spot and with the assistance of a Sgt and a Spr, despite the fact that there was a severe air raid on at the time they uncovered the bomb, placed it in a lorry and drove the dangerous cargo to a safer spot where he finally defuzed it and rendered it safe."

The whole operation was carried out under constant air raid conditions.

* * * * * * * * * * * *

Lieut E R (Eric) Raby, who was commanding 75 and 76 Independent B D Sections had dealt with a 250kg bomb, fitted with a (17) fuze, which was ticking. He was able to remove the fuze, but before he had a chance to remove the gaine, it exploded in his hands causing severe injuries.

* * * * * * * * * * * *

Because of the number of bombs to be dealt with by the B D Companies, it was agreed that a system of priorities should be established. The fact that the Germans had a 'Long Delay Fuze' which could be set to explode any time up to around 9∅ hours after it had been dropped, it was laid down, for safety reasons, that work would not commence on any bomb until four days had elapsed. Unless the circumstance required otherwise. The 'otherwise' was when an explosion would damage the War Effort.

In such cases, a Category 'A1' was allocated, which meant that work commenced immediately - *regardless of loss of life to Bomb Disposal personnel.*

Unexploded bombs were dealt with according to the allocated 'Categories' or priorities, which were;-

A.1. Immediate Disposal essential. Detonation of bomb 'in situ' cannot be accepted on any terms.

A.2. Immediate disposal essential. Bomb may, if the situation demands it, be detonated 'in situ'.

B.   Rapid disposal urgent, less urgent than 'A'.

C.   Not necessarily calling for immediate attention.

D.   May be dealt with as convenient. (Bombs falling in open country usually came into this category.)

* * * * * * * * * * * *

Lieut G R (Rex) Ovens was working on an incident in London in 194∅. It was not very pleasant, to say the least.

He tells of how the bomb had penetrated to about 2∅ feet and had broken into the side of one of the old London brick built sewers. *The stench was pretty terrific and I recall the NCO in charge saying that the air was so foul that you had to 'fart' to get some fresh air ! The bomb was in an awkward position. I had to lay prone to get at the fuze. After a few minutes I had to go up top for some fresh air.*

As I cleared my lungs, I was told by my NCO that an officer wished to speak to me. A dapper and immaculate little Captain told me that their Majesties were in the area and would like to speak to a Bomb Disposal Officer. It was then that he got a whiff of the sewers, clinging to me and he moved discreetly away from me. I told him that once I had dealt with this bomb, I had other priority incidents to deal with. He agreed that I shouldn't delay my programme, so I didn't meet their Majesties. Although, later, I did meet the then Duke of Gloucester.

* * * * * * * * * * * *

A 250kg bomb fell in the Ryvita factory in Birmingham, penetrating to a depth of 32 feet. During the digging of the shaft, at 17 feet, they came across a strata of old Calcium Carbide. One man was overcome by fumes and had to be rescued, at great personal risk by Sgt Edward Laing, who then continued to remove the remainder of the Carbide, thus allowing work to progress. Once the bomb was reached he had to lie full length alongside the bomb digging with a trowel to uncover the fuze and then remove it.

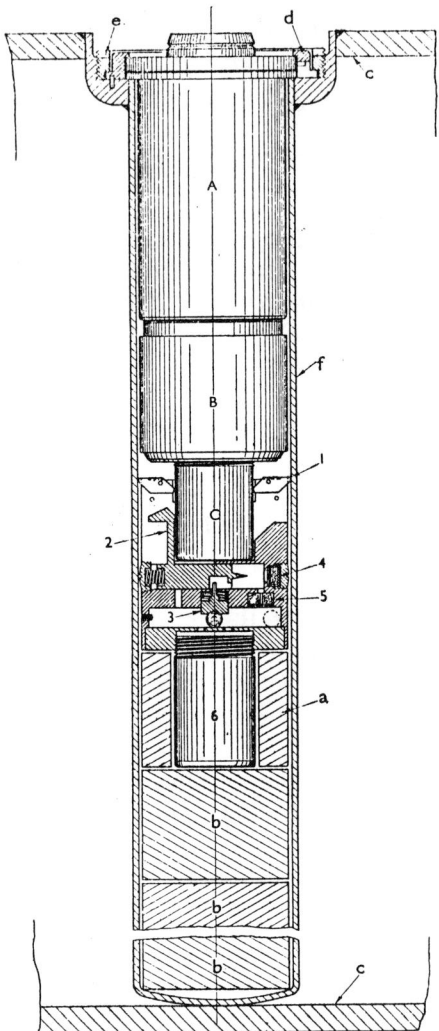

Fuze Pocket fitted with No. [17] Fuze and Zus 40

A. Electrical portion of No. [17] fuze.
B. Clock of No. [17] fuze.
C. Gaine of No. [17] fuze.

1. Knife-edge.
2. Spring-loaded trigger member with needle striker.
3. Spring-loaded locking detent, with retaining ball. ⎫
4. Detonator (ignitory). ⎬ Zus 40.
5. Booster pellet. ⎭
6. Gaine.

a. Picric ring.
b. Picric pellets.
c. Bomb casing.

d. Fuze locating ring.
e. Fuze locking ring.
f. Fuze pocket casing.

28

Chapter Three

AUGUST 1940

This view, from an 'other rank' level was written by then a L/Cpl, C.E. Brinton who was, subsequently, awarded the British Empire Medal. He writes;- *" I was posted from No 2 TBRE (Training Battalion, Royal Engineers) to 61 B D Section, at their HQ in Leeds, towards the end of August 1940. We were immediately entrained to London, where we were driven to the Duke of Yorks Barracks at Chelsea. That weekend, the Blitz started on London. We spent Sunday settling in and first thing on Monday morning I was allocated a 30 cwt truck, with a Driver and four Sappers. We were taken to a hole in the road, outside a pub called 'The Windmill' on Clapham Common. I was told to dig down until we found an unidentified object.*

None of us had had any experience or training in Bomb Disposal, so you can imagine that we were all a bit nervous. By midday, we had dug down about six feet, when a battery of Ack Ack guns opened up. We had no idea that there was a battery of 4.5 inch guns sited around the common and they were firing at a German plane which had managed to penetrate our defences. My concern was that the vibrations might set off the bomb.

From then on, we were digging up bombs from daylight to dark. Within three weeks our officer and all the NCO's, apart from myself had been killed. Many of them were killed because of a stupid action on behalf of the young, newly commissioned and inexperienced officer.

One of the sections had uncovered a 250kg bomb, which had gone through a cast iron main drainage pipe. As a result the bomb was damaged and the fuze pocket so distorted that it was impossible to remove the fuze. As it was now evening and the local ARP Warden had collected a fair sum of money from the grateful residents, thinking that they would be able to return to their homes, the Cpl decided to load the bomb on the truck and take it away. The bomb was duly loaded onto the truck and they took it back to the Duke of Yorks barracks, where they left it and went for their evening meal.

When an officer saw the bomb in the back of the truck, he decided that it should be taken immediately to the 'Bomb Cemetery' in Regents Park. The truck driver asked to be excused, as he had a date with his girlfriend. The officer agreed and drove the truck himself. As the bomb was so badly damaged, it was thought not to present any danger, the whole section jumped on the truck, 'For the ride' and a drink in the Local on the way back. There was no coming back. The bomb exploded whilst they were all on it !

For many weeks, I was dealing with bombs of all sizes including at least three with clockwork fuzes. I remember two incidents in Croydon, about half a mile apart. One was in a built up area whilst the other was in a school playground. I visited the one in the built up area first only to find that they had not yet reached the bomb, so I went to the second bomb. I was only in the next street when there was a huge explosion. I knew, instinctively, that it was the bomb I had just left. The incredible thing is that the driver who 'had a date' and thus wasn't killed earlier, was on that job. Although he was with that working party, he suddenly saw a Warden walking in the 'Evacuation Area'. He rushed up to him and escorted him out of the area. It was just as they reached the barrier, that the bomb exploded.

We were digging in a side street just off the main thoroughfare through Camberwell and had uncovered the bomb at 30ft. We had a set of shear legs over the shaft, which was used to lower a large bucket, for the removal of the soil. I was just being lowered in the bucket to deal with the fuze, I was about five or six feet above the bomb when a German aircraft started dropping bombs. The men on the lowering rope let go and I fell with a 'Bang' on the bomb. I thought my last minute had come. There followed a number of explosions as the stick of bombs exploded. With each explosion the bomb on which I rested shook. Then there was 'quiet'. A few minutes later two heads appeared at the top of the shaft and a tremulous voice enquired "Are you alright" ? My answer was unprintable !

When we had an officer all he had in the way of equipment was a doctor's stethoscope, a two pronged fuze discharger and a fuze key. When I dealt with a bomb I only had a fuze key. I just unscrewed the locking ring and took out the fuze, regardless of what it was. I must have had a Guardian Angel ! When I left 61 B D Section at the end of 1941, there were just five of us left, out of the original thirty and I was now a Sgt.

Sometime later, we were issued with an 'Electrical Stethoscope'. It was a bit 'Heath Robinsonish', in that the microphone was in a round brass barrel, with the electrics inside and a brass probe on the end, which had to be held against the fuze. I remember using it for the first time, when I had a call "It's ticking" ! I said "Hang on a minute, I think it is my hand shaking". When I held it with both hands it stopped ticking !

After leaving B D, I went to the Middle East, where I cleared minefields around El Alamien, took part in the invasion of Sicily, came back to England and joined the 'D Day' landings in Normandy."

* * * * * * * * * * * *

On 15th August a Captain C G (Charles) Stewart was called to a number of incidents in the region of the Kingston By Pass, between Malden, Coombe, Merton and Morden where some 17 UXB's had been reported. Seven

31

of these had fallen in the works of the Young Accumulator Company. Two were skilfully removed from under the foundations of the main building, whilst two others had passed through a large acid tank. The acid had, in fact, penetrated the ground around the bombs. It was feared that they might be detonated by the action of the corrosive acid whist work was in progress in addition to the hazard of the acid itself to the personnel involved. In spite of all this, the bombs were reached and immunized.

Another bomb, a 500kg, fell through the "Cricketer's Arms' at Mitcham and penetrated to a depth of twenty eight feet. The pub was adjacent to the Fire Brigade HQ and the Town Hall and its presence also interrupted traffic between Reigate and Brighton. Captain Stewart remained on site for two days, even though he had been advised to take sick leave as he was on the verge of a mental breakdown due to strain and overwork. He was awarded the George Medal for his devotion to duty.

* * * * * * * * * * *

On 13th August Capt H (Harry) Mitchell was given a list of UXB's to deal with. His first was a 250kg with a new type of fuze - a long delayed action, which contained a clockwork mechanism. It was the first he had encountered and there was no information about such a fuze. He decided to disarm the bomb, by removing the fuze, so that it could be sent for research. He was awarded the George Medal. There were many incidents of officers coming across a new fuze and removing it for research. There is, however, no record of those who died trying to do the self same thing.

* * * * * * * * * * * *

At 21.30hrs on 14th August, in Sunderland, Sgt Francis Smith with a section of No 14 B D Company, set to work on a reported UXB in Laing's Shipyard, close to a battery of radial drilling machines. The bomb proved to be a 250kg, when it was found at a depth of 15 feet. Unfortunately it had come to rest under two corrugated sheets of one eighth of an inch thick steel. By the time they reached the bomb another heavy raid was in progress and the factory workers had taken cover. However, he and L/Sgt P N Denison plus two Sappers continued to work, by the light of a motorcycle headlight, screened by a greatcoat. Whilst they worked, bombs were falling as well as shrapnel from our own A.A. guns. However, their persistence was rewarded by reaching and immunising the bomb by 08.00hrs the following morning.

* * * * * * * * * * * *

Also on 14th August, at Lyndhurst, a 500kg bomb fell in the Electricity Depot and failed to explode. Lieut C R (Charles) Wood, who commanded 50 and 51 Independent B D Sections went to the site and realising the danger to civilians and valuable property in the area - apart from the loss of the electrical supply, should it explode - set to work with Sapper Williams. When they reached the bomb it proved to have a (17) long delay fuze, which Lieut Wood managed to extract for research purposes. Whilst not the first fuze to be recovered, little was known, at the time, of its danger. He was awarded the George Medal.

Sapper James Williams assisted Lieut Wood at this incident and he, too, was awarded the George Medal. Unfortunately he was wounded at another incident on 8th September.

* * * * * * * * * * * *

On 17th August 1940. Lieut E W Reynolds, who was commanding 101 and 102 B D Sections of No 8 B D Company, went to a reported UXB in a council estate at Congresbury. When his section reached a depth of 17 feet he found that the bomb had a fuze about which he had received no instruction. Finding that the traffic had been suspended and that the inhabitants had been cleared out of their homes, he removed the fuze, which was found to have a clockwork delayed action.

The risk he took was great and merit of his action was the greater for the lack of exact knowledge of the type of fuze with which he was dealing.

* * * * * * * * * * * *

On 18th August 1940, L/Sgt W J Button, of 48 B D Section of No 6 B D Company, was working on an unexploded bomb on the Southern Railway line near Hook station. As it was holding up mainline traffic to the West, the bomb had been given a Category 'A' and the section had started work immediately on receiving the UXB report.

Although Sgt Button knew full well that because of the time already spent on the excavation, the bomb could explode at any moment, he continued to work with his section, showing great coolness.

The bomb did, eventually explode, killing five men, throwing Sgt Button a considerable distance. Fortunately he survived, collecting the remainder of his section and checking up on their injuries, before reporting the incident to his Section Officer.

L/Sgt Button was awarded the George Cross for his bravery.

* * * * * * * * * * * *

Also on 18th August a 250kg bomb fell in a factory, when it was reached, it was found to contain a long delay fuze which was, in fact, ticking. In spite of this both Lieut H A (Harold) Manser and Sgt William Jones, at great risk to themselves, continued to uncover and remove the fuze. After a considerable time they were successful and the bomb was rendered harmless. For their cool courage, with a high expectancy of sudden death, they were both awarded the George Medal.

* * * * * * * * * * * *

On 26th August, 2/Lieut W L Andrews, who was commanding 22 and 23 B D Sections of No 2 B D Company based in Balham, was trying to extract a fuze from a UXB which had been uncovered by the men of one of his sections. It was a new fuze and he was trying to recover it so that it could be sent to the Research Dept, but he was having some difficulty.

After withdrawing the fuze about 1½ inches, the fuze dropped back into the fuze pocket as if actuated by magnetism or a spring. Removal was attempted several times, without success.

He then sent his section to a place of safety and, after tying a piece of cord to the ring of the fuze discharger (Crabtree), he retired some yards before pulling the cord. When he did so, the bomb exploded. He was still blown a considerable distance and, in spite of his precautions, two of his men suffered splinter wounds.

Throughout the whole procedure, Lieut Andrews displayed great coolness and keenness in the interest of the service.

He was awarded the George Cross for his gallantry and coolness in action.

* * * * * * * * * * * *

Cpl William Bean of 77 B D Section, No 10 B D Company, based at Manchester, was one of very few junior NCO's to be awarded a George Medal, for Bomb Disposal Operations. His was awarded for quick thinking, coolness and example to the men under his command in that on 31st August, at Middleton, several high explosive bombs fell near a thickly populated area, eight of which failed to explode.

Digging began to recover the bombs, one of which had fallen in the bank of the railway line. After digging a few feet bad ground was encountered, which slowed down the work. However, by his leadership all the bombs were recovered and several hundred people, who had been evacuated, were able to return to their homes.

* * * * * * * * * * * *

Just a week later 2/Lieut E E (Eric) Talbot, who commanded 103 B D Section of No 8 B D Company was in charge of excavating a UXB on another railway line just outside Longhor station. He had been there for the the twelve and a half hours it had taken to dig down to the bomb and when it had been brought to the surface, he realised that it had a delay type fuze and ordered his men to a safe distance, whilst he examined it.

As it appeared to be of a new type, Lieut Talbot decided to remove it to a place where it could do no damage if it exploded. Still keeping his men under cover, he carried the bomb on his shoulders for some 200 yards to a 'safe' spot.

From start to finish there was a risk of the bomb exploding and he set a fine example of devotion to duty, for which he was awarded 'The Medal of the Military Division of the Most Excellent Order of the British Empire, for Gallantry. (E.G.M), which was later converted to the George Cross.

* * * * * * * * * * * *

On the 28th August, ten bombs were dropped on Hartshorne. They were high explosive of which two failed to explode. Capt J R F (John) McCartney and his 17 men started work on the one at Boffey's Farm. It had penetrated to a depth of 26 feet and digging was dangerous as it was close to the foundations of the building. They dug through various stratas of ground. First soil, the sub soil, shaly clay, a seam of coal, some four feet thick and, finally, pottery clay. It took just a week to reach and render the bomb safe.

The second bomb was close to the Bull's Head and had penetrated to some 28 feet. In this instance the digging problem was 'water', which meant that the walls of the shaft were in continual danger of collapsing. Regardless of this the men displayed exceedingly high spirits and grim determination. For this, and other operations, Capt McCartney was awarded the George Medal. Shortly after, Capt McCartney was promoted to Major and took command of the newly formed No 3 B D Company.

* * * * * * * * * * * *

Lieut D S F (Douglas) Rayner went to an unspecified but important aeroplane factory, which had been closed down because of the presence of six unexploded bombs. He set his men working on all six bombs and within half a day they had been uncovered and he had defused all of them.

Two days later he removed a 250kg bomb from another factory. This one containing a ticking (17) fuze. As with many other bombs, which had passed through concrete, the fuze pocket had been damaged and he had the greatest difficulty in removing it, having to resort to the use of a Marlinespike. It took thirty five minutes to remove the fuze which could have detonated at any time. For these incidents he was awarded the George Medal

* * * * * * * * * * * *

It is no wonder that the life expectancy of a B D Officer, at this time, was just

SIXTEEN WEEKS.

* * * * * * * * * * * *

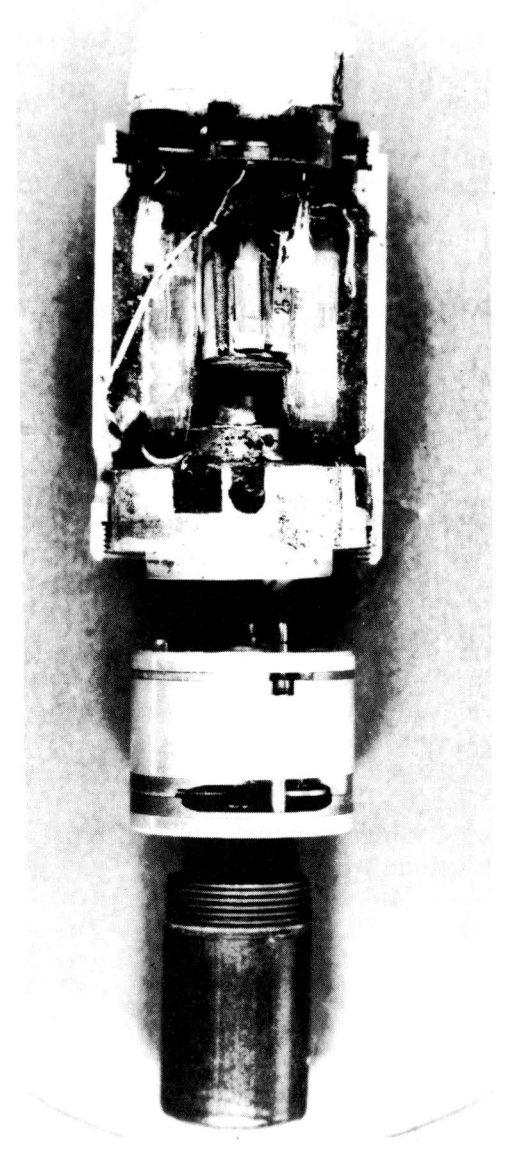

A sectionalised (17) fuze, out of it's case, showing the clock mechanism and Gaine.

Photo courtesy of Capt A F J Hannaford

Chapter Four

SEPTEMBER 1940

On 3rd September 1940, Lieut E W Reynolds went to deal with a large bomb which had fallen in Temple Street, Bristol on the night of 1st September. After some clearance, a 250kg bomb was found amongst the debris. He then discovered that it was fuzed with a (17) fuze, which was ticking. According to orders, at that time, he applied to Regional Headquarters for instructions, suggesting that the sooner it was dealt with the better and that he was willing so to do. In view of the damage to property, which would have been caused by an explosion of such a large bomb and especially of the possible effect on the public morale, permission was given and Lieut Reynolds immediately extracted the fuze and rendered the bomb safe.

The risk in removing the fuze was considerable. Many officers were killed at that time because they removed a (17) fuze, which had a booby trap underneath.

For this action and his previous efforts on 17th August, Lieut Reynolds was awarded the George Cross.

* * * * * * * * * * * *

The most publicised award of the George Cross, partly because it was the first to be awarded and partly because of its location was that of Lieut R (Robert) Davies. Who was commanding 16 and 17 B D Sections of No 5 B D Company, based in Acton.

He was in charge of the party detailed to recover an unexploded bomb which had fallen in the vicinity of St Paul's Cathedral. Preferably, without exploding it !

So conscious was he of the imminent danger to the Cathedral that, regardless of the personal risk, he spared neither himself nor his men in their efforts to locate the bomb.

After unremitting effort. during which all ranks knew that an explosion might occur at any moment, the bomb was successfully extricated.

In order to shield his men from further danger, Lieut Davies then carried out the disposal of the bomb.

Sapper George Wylie, who assisted Lieut Davies throughout the whole time was also awarded the George Cross for his untiring energy, courage and disregard for danger, which were an outstanding example to his comrades.

Sgt James Wilson who was the senior NCO of the team and L/Cpl Herbert Leigh, who also worked on the bomb were both awarded the British Empire Medal for their bravery.

All four awards were published in the London Gazette in November 1940

The following appeared in The Times on 16th September 1940;-

No 5 BOMB DISPOSAL COMPANY R.E.

Bomb by St Paul's Removed

Bomb Disposal Men's courage

"The high explosive bomb which fell near St Paul's Cathedral on Wednesday was removed safely yesterday by experts. For the first time for several days traffic was allowed through the area and it is expected that business premises which have been closed will be allowed to reopen today.

For the first time in many, many years there was not service in the Cathedral yesterday morning.

For the last three days a bomb disposal section under Lieut R Davies had been trying to remove the bomb, which had entered the road in Dean's Yard, close to the West end of the cathedral. It was found that a 6 inch gas main had been fractured and three men were gassed at an early stage. The main had caught fire and after the gas had been turned off, the bomb disposal section had to dig 27 ft 6 in into the subsoil before they found the bomb. It proved to be a ton in weight and described as about 8 ft long. With great difficulty it was drawn up with special tackle and two lorries were required to haul it out of the hole. The streets were cleared for a long distance and the bomb was driven by Lieut Davies to Hackney Marshes where it was blown up. The explosion caused a 100 ft crater and rattled windows and in one case loosened plaster in home far away on the marshes.

The Ministry of Home Security, in a description of the work, said: 'Only courage and tenacity of the officer, his NCO's and men prevented St Paul's from being levelled to the ground.' "

At the end of September 1970, some thirty years later, Lieut Davies's George Cross was auctioned at Spinks, reaching a figure of £2,100 - a world record price for a military medal.

In 1977, Sapper George Wylie put his George Cross up for auction. The Imperial War Museum declined to purchase it, but out of the blue, the City Merchant Bankers Charterhouse Japhet, whose officers at Paternoster Row looked out on St Pauls's bought the medal privately and presented it to St Pauls's Cathedral, where it is on permanent display in the Treasury in the Crypt.

* * * * * * * * * * * *

Lieut Colonel A D Merriman was awarded the George Cross, for his work in connection with unexploded bombs, when working as an Experimental Officer of the

Department of Scientific Research, prior to joining the Royal Engineers.

He removed the fuzes from the very first German bombs which fell unexploded on the Shetland Isles in December 1939. Subsequently, he disarmed bombs which had new and unknown types of fuze. Nearly all were delayed action fitted with anti handling devices.

In September 1940, he with Dr H J Gough, the Director General of Scientific Research, tackled the disarming of a bomb which had fallen in Regent Street, in London. Their efforts to stop the delayed action mechanism failed and eventually, Merriman stayed and helped the task of removing the main charge from the bomb.

This was accomplished with the mechanism ticking away. When most of the explosive had been removed the bomb exploded, causing little damage to the surrounding property.

* * * * * * * * * * * *

September 1940 was a very busy month. On 14th a large bomb fell in an important factory. Evacuation supervised by Sgt Gibson was begun, during which time another bomb which had fallen nearby exploded.

Despite the knowledge that the bomb upon which he was working could be of a similar type he persevered until the bomb was uncovered. It was then that an unusual hissing sound was heard coming from the bomb. He immediately sent all his men away to a safe distance and then set to work on the fuze, which he extracted safely.

His prompt action and courageous action saved a very dangerous situation.

He was awarded the George Cross.

* * * * * * * * * * * *

On 14th September a bomb was reported to have fallen in the centre of a large machine shop engaged in

42

work of National Importance. Captain R (Ralph) Chalkley of the Royal Army Ordnance Corps, attached to the 1st Anti Aircraft Division went to the scene.

With the aid of a hacksaw he cut through the top of a 250lb Incendiary bomb and, by doing so, was able to remove the bomb from the concrete in which it was embedded.

His action was the more outstanding as he had little knowledge of the types of enemy bombs and the removal of them was not part of his duties. His prompt and courageous action resulted in work recommencing with confidence in a very short space of time. He was awarded the George Medal for his bravery.

* * * * * * * * * * * *

On 16th September a large unexploded bomb was reported at Lord Stanhope's residence at Chevening, where Lady Stanhope was lying seriously ill and unable to be moved. Lieut F R (Francis) Martin was detailed for the job. Having recently lost four men on a similar bomb, he decided to recover the bomb himself and not risk other lives. After many hours of solitary digging he reached the bomb - at 04.00 hrs the next day. - He extracted the fuze - which was still ticking - He undoubtedly saved the life of Lady Stanhope, at the very great risk of his own. A well deserved George Medal.

* * * * * * * * * * * *

Vickers Supermarine Factory at Woolston was hit on 26th September. Lieut R C B Maitland and his men started work just four hours after the 250kg bomb had been dropped. It was found at a depth of four feet, having been slowed down and considerably damaged by the concrete through which it passed. The fuzes were unidentifiable and the fuze pockets distorted, rendering removal impossible, in spite of the use of hammer and cold chisel. The filling plate was removed and the bomb was found to be filled with cast TNT. There was no other alternative that to remove the bomb to the demolition ground. Lieut Maitland drove the vehicle.

At 17.00 hrs on the following day he went to the Gas Works in Southampton, to deal with another Category 'A' bomb. The whole plant had been shut down and the gas was urgently required for local war production factories. On arrival he found two bombs, both 250kg. Fortunately, they were both fitted with (15) fuzes which were removed by 20.00 hrs

On the following day he was found, at 14.00 hrs, in the Electricity Power Station. The bomb had only been dropped a few hours earlier. A 250kg bomb, with an unrecognisable fuze. A hammer and chisel was resorted to again to remove it. A very dangerous operation, when one doesn't know the type of fuze one is working on.

He was extremely lucky, when working on a bomb. He and his section started work at 09.00 hrs, knocked off for a meal at 12.15 hrs. The bomb exploded exactly 15 minutes later, completely destroying the nearby road.

In November they had been digging down to a bomb and were down some fifteen feet when, again, they knocked off. The bomb exploded when he was just ten yards away.

* * * * * * * * * * * *

Like Col Archer, Lieut C H (Cliff) Green GM, was a 'pre war Territorial', only already in the Corps of Royal Engineers. At the outbreak of the war he received a 'direct' Commission and was posted to 718 General Construction Company, RE. The O.C. was Major W G Henry MC. This unit was recruited by Lieut Green's employer, from his workers and he had nominated him as one of his junior officers.

The Company formed up at Chatham, then going to a training camp at Launceston for their initial Military and Engineer Training, which is where he joined them. On completion of their training, the sections went out on detachment to various locations to construct pill boxes and other defences, the Company HQ going to Wadebridge.

On 21st September, Lieut Green and another officer were hurriedly informed that they were to leave immediately for an 'RAF Armaments Course', at RAF Manby, in Lincolnshire. They were quite pleased for they knew of straffing by planes of people on defence works and they thought they would be able to defend themselves against such attacks.

The Course opened with the Chief Instructor saying; " Good morning, gentlemen, welcome to Bomb Disposal Course No 1 ! Or, in other words, what goes up must come down." There was a long quiet silence. Then the room erupted. The whole class wanted to know what Bomb Disposal was.

They learnt what was known about German bombs and fuzes, which was very little, how to detonate them and basic explosive training. They did the same for British Bombs and fuzes and very general information on digging for bombs and safety precautions. On the Saturday they were dispersed and to their astonishment were despatched to Tunbridge Wells, where, it seems their unit had been moved. Owing to the railway being bombed they didn't arrive at their destination until late on Sunday.

They found that their sections had been reformed with additional men and officers posted in to form ten B.D Sections, plus an HQ comprising of an O.C., 2IC, Intelligence Officer, Transport Officer and a Q.M. (Quartermaster).

On the following morning, they checked their stores, were given explosives, sandbags, etc. and sent off to deal with their first bombs.

Lieut Green found Bombs Nos 1 and 2, in the playing field of a school in Gravesend. Instructions, at the time, were that the fuzes should not be removed, but having identified the fuze and made a note of all the marking, it was to be demolished in situ. Sandbag walls were built to guide the blast away from the buildings. This was done and the resultant craters were left for the local Council to fill in. Which was not until sometime after, Later, he discovered that both bombs, which were 250kg, had been fitted with Long Delay fuzes.

The next was in Bowater Paper Mills, close to the waters edge of the River Thames. So close, that they could only work between tides. It turned out to be a Flam 250 incendiary bomb. Had it been a heavy bomb, they would have never found it. They were all sorry to leave as they had meals in the Works Canteen and were billeted in the Staff Quarters. Needless to say the men were getting on very well with the female staff !

The fourth bomb must have been dropped from a low level. It came down in the road, hit an obstruction which turned it into a space between two houses coming to rest some twenty yards away in the back garden, with it's nose sticking out of the ground and the fuze visible. It had been badly damaged and was unidentifiable. With a hammer and cold chisel he managed to undo the locking ring. Unfortunately, when he withdrew it and the locating ring, the fuze head came away as well. He used the Doctor's Stethoscope, with which he had been issued, but could not hear any ticking. - They were unreliable, anyway ! - The working party were told to move themselves and all the equipment to a safe distance and the Police were informed.

Using a hammer, a screwdriver and cold chisel, he was able to lever the remains of the fuze out of the fuze pocket. It turned out to be a (17) Long Delay fuze. The gaine was removed (Standard practice) and the fuze fired ten minutes later.

For this incident and many others Lieut Green was awarded the George Medal. Sapper Carter was also awarded it, for his continual support.

* * * * * * * * * * * *

46

On 4th September, Lieut D H (Daniel) Ramage, who had both 81 and 82 Independent B D Sections under his command, was called to a factory of Pilkington Bros, in St Helens. The bomb had penetrated to a depth of twelve feet and had been so damaged by it's passage through the concrete floor, that it was impossible to remove the fuze. As the presence of the bomb was holding up vital war production, he decided on a novel approach, in that he unscrewed the filler cap and removed the TNT filling until he could reach the fuze pocket to withdraw it. For his conspicuous courage, coolness and ability to adapt to various situations, he was awarded the George Medal.

* * * * * * * * * * * *

Lieut C E (Charles) Davies of No 23 B D Company, based at Winchester, joined B D in August 1940. Within a year he had dealt with some four hundred bombs. Thirty five of which had been classified as 'A'. One these occurred on 21st September, when at 10.30hrs two 50kg bombs fell in the works of the Hawker Aircraft Company. By 14.00hrs Lieut Davies arrived and dealt the first bomb, which had not penetrated the concrete floor of the factory. He was thus able to remove it to a crater in a nearby airfield.

The second bomb had penetrated the concrete and an excavation was commenced. It continued throughout the night and at 08.00hrs the following day the bomb was reached. Both bombs were fitted with (17) long delay fuzes. The bomb which had been taken to the airfield exploded whilst the squad was digging for the second bomb.

By his bravery and that of his men, who continued to work, knowing that they might be blown up any minute, 25 very precious aircraft were saved.

* * * * * * * * * * * *

Bombs seemed to have a preference for coming to rest, unexploded in sewers. The two following stories both relate to such a resting place.

In September a large bomb fell in Monk Street, Woolwich, behind the Town hall and near the Southern Railway station. No definite information could be obtained as to the exact time it had fallen, but in view of the proximity to the mainline railway it was decided to start work on it immediately. On uncovering the bomb, it was found to have two (17) fuzes. At the time they had only one 'Clockstopper', so it was decided to remove the fuzes. Unfortunately, whilst the officer was doing so the bomb exploded and he was seriously injured. A spell in hospital and sick leave followed.

In the following month - It must have been a short sick leave - he was back dealing with a bomb which had fallen in the Southern Outface Sewer. In this case he had decided to explode the bomb in situ. Having lit the fuze and retired to a safe distance he suddenly saw an old lady emerge from a totally unexpected quarter, into the danger area. He immediately ran to her and was successful in reaching her and taking her to a place of safety before the bomb exploded.

* * * * * * * * * * * * *

Corporal John Jelley, was in 8 section of No 4 B D Company. At 01.00 hrs on 19th September, a large bomb fell in Theatre Street of Norwich. A thickly populated area, which was immediately evacuated. A similar bomb which had been dropped at the same time, exploded at 12.45 hrs that day. As the bomb was not categorised as 'A', it was left for the 'safe' period of four days, before work commenced. Work thus began on 23rd at 09.00 hrs. The bomb, weighing 880lbs had penetrated to a depth of twenty two feet and was found to be fitted with a new type of clockwork fuze. Knowing that the bomb might explode at any time and with total disregard for his personal safety he carried on, without interruption, until the bomb was loaded on a lorry and taken away. He insisted on going insisted on going with the bomb, whilst it was being transported. For his bravery and devotion to duty and leadership he was awarded the George Medal.

* * * * * * * * * * * *

On the morning of 21st September 1940, at about 10.30hrs the Hawker Aircraft factory at Weybridge was attacked. Three bombs were dropped, two of which exploded causing slight damage. The third, a 250kg, penetrated the factory roof, passed through a wall at the end of the building and came to rest on a concrete driveway outside the erecting shed. Had it exploded, it would have done irreparable damage to the building and the aircraft inside.

The 1st Canadian Pioneer Battalion. RCE, were stationed nearby and they were asked if they had a Bomb Disposal section with them which, unfortunately they did not, neither was a British Army Bomb Disposal unit immediately available. So, Lieut J M S Patten, who had had no training or experience of unexploded bombs decided to have a go the bomb. Having looked at it, he decided that he did not have sufficient knowledge to remove the fuze, so he decided to tow it away from where it lay. A truck was brought up close and a cable was connected to it and the bomb. By this time, the Acting Company Commander, Captain D W Cunnington had arrived. Between them they managed to get the bomb on an old sheet of corrugated iron. Capt Cunnington cleared a path of all debris, to ensure a smooth journey for the bomb and Lieut Patten drove the truck towing the bomb slowly towards a crater created during an earlier raid.

The bomb exploded the following morning.

Lieut Patten was awarded the George Cross for his cool assessment of the situation and the action he took. Capt Cunnington was awarded the George Medal for showing complete disregard for his personal safety.

* * * * * * * * * * * *

In September and October, Lieut C N (Neville) Newitt had four lucky escapes. His first was a Category 'A' bomb, upon which they commenced work immediately it was reported. They worked throughout the day and, shortly after knocking off for a meal, the bomb exploded.

The second bomb was in Regent Street. They had got down to the bomb and were removing the TNT filling by steaming it out, when the bomb exploded. Fortunately, Lieut Newitt had maintained safety precautions and no one was killed or injured.

In October they dug up a 250kg bomb at the National Gallery. It was removed from the site, to apply a new method of immunisation. On arrival at the new location, they unloaded the bomb and went for their lunch. It exploded a few minutes after they left.

His section removed another bomb from Pall Mall, took it to the demolition site, where it exploded a few minutes later.

This sort of action, by Section Officers, was commonplace in that little was known about German bomb fuzes and they were required for research. In addition, most officers wanted to preserve the property which would be destroyed if the bombs exploded in situ.

* * * * * * * * * * * *

By the end of September there were well over three thousand unexploded bombs waiting immunisation and removal. It thus put a strain on the housing departments of local councils. It also put a strain on the Bomb Disposal Subaltern who, when he came across a (17) fuze was told to explode 'in situ'. This, of course, led to more houses being damaged and made uninhabitable. Conscious of this situation, many young officers would risk their own lives, by having the bomb loaded on the back of a truck and driving it to an area where it could be exploded without doing any damage to property. Lieut H A (Henry) Grover was one such subaltern, driving a truck with a ticking (17) from Brentford to Syon Park, for which he was awarded the George Medal.

* * * * * * * * * * * *

Also in September, Lieut Manser, who had already been recommended for the George Medal for his earlier bravery, dealt with another 250kg bomb with a (17) long delay fuze. This time he was assisted by Sgt S E J (Sidney) Thorne. The conditions under which the operation was carried out was such that Sgt Thorne was awarded the George Medal. Unfortunately, Lieut Manser was killed shortly after with another NCO.

The H.Q. of No 16 B D Company at Mt St Alban, Christchurch near Newport (Mon).
Photo courtesy of Capt A F J Hannaford

Lieut W L Andrews with some of his men, recovering an, as yet, unidentified bomb.
Note the 'non issue wash tub' being used to remove the earth from the unsupported hole
they have dug.
Photo courtesy of Mrs S Brown.

52

Chapter Five

OCTOBER 1940

One of the most unusual - and fastest - disposal of a UXB was carried out by Capt S (Sam) Garside. He and his Sgt went to the site of a reported UXB, where they found a very clean 'trace' of the bomb. (The path it makes as it goes through the ground.) It was a 500kg and thus the diameter was around 24 inches. Capt Garside probed down this hole in the ground until he came to the tail fins, they were in reach and so he tied a rope round them, returned to the surface and between them they were able to pull the metal out of the hole. This left a clear shaft right down to the bomb.

Using a long pole, he was able to push an explosive charge down to the bomb. They then exploded the bomb. It cleared the site and not one shovel full of earth had been lifted !

For this and many other 'episodes', not all as unusual, he was awarded the George Medal.

* * * * * * * * * * * *

Major H J L Barefoot, who was Officer Commanding No 4 B D Company in the very early days, was awarded his George Cross for various operations ranging from May to October 1940. He was a pioneer of Bomb Disposal.

He dealt with the first unexploded bomb found on mainland Britain and by his disregard of personal safety, very valuable information was obtained.

He experimented with all types of bombs. With a Naval Officer he worked on the first suspended Parachute Magnetic Mine. For two hours he clung to the mine to secure it in a safe position. At the time of this act the Bomb Disposal Authorities had very little knowledge of the mechanism of these mines and much was learnt at this stage.

When necessary, he ignored the safety period, especially when clearing an important railway line.

His bravery and devotion to duty did much to maintain a high standard in his Company.

* * * * * * * * * * * *

Also in 4 B D Company, a Lieut E J (Evelyn) Halsted-Handby, commanded 8 B D Section. As a result of a raid on the night of 18/19th September on Norwich, the city was left with two large unexploded bombs. One in Theatre Street and the other in Mousehold. As he approached the latter at 11.30hrs that morning it exploded, creating a crater some thirty feet across. Fortunately, he was not injured but, in the knowledge that the one in Theatre street might explode at any time, he and his section set to work on 23rd. They were to dig down to a depth of twenty feet before reaching the bomb. It was found to have a new design of clockwork fuze. Fortunately, he was able to remove the fuze, without an explosion and the centre of the city of Norwich was able to return to what was 'normal' for wartime Britain.

* * * * * * * * * * * *

A bomb fell in the Royal Ordnance Factory, Bishopston on 2nd October. Given an 'A.1.' category, work was commenced immediately. The soil was blue clay and difficult to dig, let alone 'timber'. Clay was later to be recognised as 'problem' when digging for a UXB as we were very rarely able to assess where the bomb had come to rest. In this incident, it took the digging of three shafts and all of fifty one days to immunise and recover, at a depth of 34 feet with an 'offset' of 16 feet.

Lieut W A (William, known as 'Butch') Feather was in B D right from the start, in No 4 B D Company, based at Bury St Edmunds, although at the time in question he was at Hornchurch and, at times, worked under very heavy raid conditions.

On 21st August, he went to eleven reported UXBs, all 50kg, which had fallen just outside the Royal Naval Mine Depot, in which loaded sea mines were stored. The close proximity of the loaded mines did not deter him and for two days he supervised the working parties digging down to five bombs which presented the greatest hazard to the explosives. One of the five bombs was fitted with a long delayed action fuze, which he was able to remove before it detonated.

On the night of 9/10th September he went to ten category 'A' bombs which had dropped in the works of the Explosives and Chemical Products Company, in Harwich. He discovered that there were three 500kg bombs, whilst the remainder were all 50kg. The majority of the bombs were within 50 yards of one ton of stored Gunpowder. He and his men worked for days under constant air attack and it was only due to his tenacity and leadership that the work was completed, all the bombs immunised and that work restarted in the factory in the minimum time.

Next month, on 28th, he was called to the Royal Air Force base at West Raynham, near King's Lynn, where 35 50kg bombs lay unexploded. All had just penetrated the surface. He and his men worked speedily to uncover the bombs, whilst he removed the (17) fuzes, although he had no previous knowledge of this type of fuze being in a 50kg. The airfield was back in operation the same day.

On the following day he was called to deal with two 250kg and one 50kg on Massingham airfield. Within three hours of them falling, he had removed the fuzes of all three - at great danger to himself - 250kg bombs fitted with (17) fuzes often had a booby trap under it, which exploded when the fuze was removed.

For these incidents and many others he was awarded the George Medal.

* * * * * * * * * * * *

Sgt George Wardrope, who had been with No 5 B D Company since the June, found himself working on a 250kg UXB which had fallen on 27th September. It had fallen some 20 yards from a railway line and just ten yards from a hospital, in Hackney. The bomb was uncovered on 5th October and proved to be fitted with a (17) fuze which was ticking. The excavation was packed with sandbags, to reduce the result of any explosion but, on 6th it was decided that it would probably be a better bet if the bomb was removed from the site as two vital services could be interrupted if the bomb exploded in situ.

The sandbags were removed and the bomb was brought to the surface, where it was still found to be ticking. The bomb was hastily placed on a truck and taken to a bomb cemetery. Further examination of the bomb showed that it was fitted with two (17) fuzes, both of which were ticking. It was left to detonate on it's own !

* * * * * * * * * * * *

At 20.20hrs on 1st October a bomb fell in the front garden of no 18 Kingsdown Road, Epsom, approximately six feet from the front door of the house and about the same distance from the boundary fence. Between that date and 10th of the month, men of 25 B D Section, under the command of Lieut C C Stewart, dug down 17 feet in solid chalk. It proved to be a 250kg bomb and it was lying in an almost vertical position. It was found to be alive and it was decided that the only method of disposal was to detonate the bomb.

Fortunately, Lieut Stewart was replaced by Lieut G R (Rex) Ovens who, with great gallantry and imminent risk to his own life succeeded in removing the filler cap of the bomb and removed the explosive contents by means of a water jet.

The above is the paraphrased recommendation, written by the Town Clerk of Epsom, recommending Lieut Ovens for an award. Unfortunately the Town Clerk was not successful and Rex did not get an award.

* * * * * * * * * * * *

On the afternoon of Thursday 3rd October 1940 three bombs were heard to drop in the vicinity of the village of Wing. On investigation by 2/Lieut P R C (Paul) Andrews of the 27th Searchlight Regiment, R A. a fourth, unexploded, bomb was found, just in the ground, with it's tail fin still showing. He considered it to be a danger to the people in the nearby house and decided to make it safe.

He pulled the bomb out of the ground and unscrewed something fitted into the nose. This proved to have nothing to do with the bombs explosive system but was the 'carrying lug'. Not having any tools with which to carry on, with the assistance of L/Bombardier Mackenzie, the bomb was carried to a safe distance from the village, roped off and warning signs placed around the area.

He later returned and was able to unscrew the Locking ring and remove the fuze and primers which *'Came out very easily !'* The bomb, now being harmless, had its base plate removed and the bomb emptied of the explosive. It was then cleaned, the tail fin put back and placed on show outside the Officers' Mess.

The award of the George Medal to 2/Lieut Andrews was not published until 22nd January 1945.

* * * * * * * * * * * *

2/Lieut A F Campbell commanded 68 B D Section of No 9 B D Company, based in Birmingham. On 17th

October 1940 he was engaged on the removal of a 250kg bomb at the Triumph Engineering Works, Coventry.

This bomb had caused the cessation of war production in two factories involving some 1,000 workers, plus the evacuation of a number of homes. For this reason he worked without rest for 48 hours until the bomb was removed.

When the bomb was finally exposed it was found to to be fitted with a delayed action fuze which it was impossible to remove. He decided to remove it to a safe place for destruction. Recognising the extreme danger involved, the bomb was loaded on a lorry and driven for a distance of a mile, during which time he was lying alongside the bomb and listening for the sound of the clockwork mechanism. They were able to reach a 'safe' area where the bomb was safely disposed of.

Unfortunately, Lieut Campbell was killed on the following day, whilst dealing with another UXB.

Sgt John Hinton was awarded the George Medal for assisting Lieut Campbell throughout the whole operation.

* * * * * * * * * * * *

Coventry, October 8th, a UXB reported in Smith's Stamping Works, engaged upon vital Air Ministry production. When the bomb was uncovered it was found to be so damaged that the fuze could not be removed, neither could the filling cap be removed, so Lieut L C (Lionel) Meynell and his NCO, of No 9 B D Company, picked up the bomb, carried it to their truck and drove it to a piece of waste ground where it detonated 45 minutes later.

A week later he was called to an R.A.F. Station where there was a reported 'Oil Incendiary' bomb. On arrival he found that it was a 250kg High Explosive bomb, fitted with a long delay fuze - which was ticking! - He immediately removed the fuze, at great risk to himself, as there could have been a booby trap underneath the fuze he removed. The award of his George Medal was published in the London Gazette on 17th December.

* * * * * * * * * * * *

On the 9th October, L/Cpl Ernest Suttle, of No 9 B D Company, in Birmingham had been in Bomb Disposal just one month when he found himself working on a 250kg bomb in the Test Laboratory and Transfer House of the English Electric Company, in Stafford. It had fallen at 11.00hrs. He and his party arrived about 15.30hrs. When it was uncovered it was found to be armed with the usual (17) and (50) fuzes. The Section Officer immunised the (50) but it was found impossible to remove the (17) fuze. So the Section Officer and L/Cpl Suttle gently removed the bomb to an area where it was safe to detonate without causing any damage.

* * * * * * * * * * * *

On 18th October, a large bomb fell into the boiler flues of the Power House at Bexley Mental Institution. Lieut J (James) Ford was tasked with the job of its removal. The bomb lay in the flue, where the temperature was considerably higher than 100 °F and where the area was polluted with gasses.

Under these difficult conditions, and in spite of the risk of the bomb exploding, Lieut Ford displayed great courage and fortitude and was fortunate enough to render the bomb safe and arrange for its removal.

For his gallantry he was awarded the George Medal.

* * * * * * * * * * * *

On 19th October, Capt T H (Tom) Sharman, of No 9 B D Company, at 03.00 hrs took his section to the G.E.C. works at Witton, whilst a heavy raid was in progress. The bomb had only fallen two and a half hours earlier. With some fast digging the bomb was uncovered and the (17) fuze removed by 09.30 the same day.

* * * * * * * * * * * *

An entry in Major W L Andrews GC diary reads;-
"*20th October, Reconnoitred a bomb at Clapham Junction. Hole of entry between the lines. Checked the hole and decided that it was a bomb hole, but there were signs of an explosion. Major Yates decided that it had exploded and created a 'camouflet'. Ten minutes after our arrival back at the Barracks, the Railway rang to say that the bomb had exploded a few minutes after we left.*"

* * * * * * * * * * * *

On 27th October, Lieut C E (Charles) Davies, not to be confused with Lieut Robert Davies, who pulled out the St Paul's bomb, went to a UXB in Onslow village, near Guildford. It was at the rear of a private house, under a sewer as well as cables and pipes carrying all the main services. It turned out to be a 250kg when he reached it and it had a (17) fuze. The removal of the fuze was found to be impossible as the fuze pocket was damaged, so it was put on a truck and driven to an area where it could be safely blown up.

On the following day, another 250kg was reported at Ormonde Road, Guildford. It had fallen in a passageway in the middle of a row of houses. It had penetrated to a depth of 16 feet, with an 'offset' of 12 feet. Which meant it had come to rest underneath one of the houses. When the bomb was, eventually, reached it was found to have both (17) and (50) fuzes

For these three incidents and a further on in May of 1941 Lieut Davies was awarded the George Medal.

* * * * * * * * * * * *

Sgt C M (Charles) Cann, of 8 B D Section, No 4 B D Company, was the first NCO of the Bomb Disposal Sections to defuze live bombs and was one of the pioneers of this work.

He undertook the delicate and dangerous work of dealing with parachute mines, irrespective of whether they had been defuzed by the Royal Navy. On one occasion he was dealing with a parachute mine, which had fallen in the back garden of one of a row of terraced houses. Whilst he was trying to immunise it, it began ticking. The fuze of a parachute mine ticks for precisely 17 seconds, before exploding. He decided that he would not be able to stop the fuze from ticking and 'ran for it' Apparently, each garden was separated by a six foot high wall. It is rumoured that Charles, who was 'tubby' at the time, was at least six gardens away before it exploded !

About the same time an Royal Naval officer had to deal with one which had finished up on the landing of a three story house. Knowing the risks, he reconnoitred an escape route. He hung a rope from the landing down the stairwell to the ground, wedged open all the doors before he started work on the mine. That also started ticking. He slid down the rope and was quite a way down the road before it exploded. He was blown further down the road and suffered a collapsed lung, but lived.

On 28th October, Sgt Cann was ordered to investigate a new type of of small anti personnel bomb, which had been dropped in considerable numbers in the Ipswich area. He, with the full knowledge of possible fatal consequences, secured a complete bomb, the mechanism of which was a 'hairsbreadth' from exploding. He dismantled and rendered the bomb harmless.

This was all done in the full knowledge that a number of Police Officers who had handled these bombs had suffered fatal results.

The valuable information was the first to be received and allowed precautionary orders to be issued.

For his bravery he was awarded the George Medal.

Later, Sgt Cann was commissioned and in 1945 was tasked with the job of providing Bomb Disposal Units with a safe method of clearing the mines laid in shingle. This he did with great ability and later that year all B D

Units working on minefield clearance were issued with 'High Pressure Water Jetting' equipment.

Unfortunately, Charles died, in the Summer of 1945, on the operating table, having a simple operation for the removal of his tonsils. Even more traumatically for his widow, their elder son, aged then about 8/10, died the following year undergoing the same operation.

* * * * * * * * * * * *

It is unusual to record the award of a George Medal to a member of the Home Guard. It is probably not a well known fact that many large factories had their own Bomb Disposal Unit, just 'in case' the Army B D Units were so stretched after a heavy raid, that they could not cope. They were called 'Auxiliary B D Units' and were rostered in to the Home Guard, but they wore the Royal Engineer Cap badge and also the treasured 'Bomb' on the sleeve of their battledress. They were trained by officers of the nearest Army Bomb Disposal Company. Many of the units did actually dig up and immunize bombs on their premises

The citation does not mention the name of the owners of the factory but it was obviously one producing 'war materials'. For example Burtons, in Leeds, the well known 'Gents outfitters' was on war work, producing uniforms for all three Services - and probably Civil defence and even the Land Army !

Platoon Officer R E (Reg) Cooke, of the Home Guard, went to deal with a 250kg bomb which fell on the factory in which he worked on 28th October 1940. When it was reached it was found to be ticking. The bomb had now been there for forty eight hours and, from experience, it was known that the bomb could explode at any time. An attempt was made to remove the fuze, but it failed and he withdrew to consider the problem.

In view of the importance of the factory it was decided to attack the fuze for a second time. This time he took a crow bar with him. In the end, it needed three people to extract the ticking fuze. This time they were partially successful, but only in pulling the fuze part way out of the bomb. It was then decided to flood the shaft and hope that the water would stop the clock. Apparently it did and the bomb was later safely removed.

Mr Cooke was awarded the George Medal. 2/Lieut R H Lee of No 9 B D Company was, as reported earlier, was also awarded the George Medal for this incident.

* * * * * * * * * * * *

Also on 28th October, Sgt Thomas Williams of No 4 B D Company, led a working party to two Category 'A' UXB's in a factory in Norwich, one of which was fitted with a ticking (17) fuze. He was successful in immunising the fuze, before it exploded and also the fuzes of the second bomb. For this incident and another in May of 1941 he was awarded the George Medal.

* * * * * * * * * * * *

A colleagues impression of Sgt Charles Cann 'legging it' away from a ticking parachute mine.

Illustration by Capt A F J Hannaford.

Chapter Six

NOVEMBER 1940

At 01.30 hours on 1st November, a 250kg bomb fell through the railway viaduct in Curzon Street, Birmingham. This was reported as a UXB to No 9 B D Company 15 minutes later. Capt A J (Alfred) Biggs set off with his Sgt to investigate. He found the bomb partially buried underneath the viaduct, where its explosion would cause much damage and seriously dislocate rail traffic for a considerable period.

He immediately set to work, soon uncovering the fuze, which was ticking. When he attempted to extract it, the locking ring jammed. Using a hammer and cold chisel, he was able to remove the base plate of the bomb and removed the explosive by means of a hosepipe and crowbar. The removal of the explosive was completed by 02.30 hours and the fuze detonated seven minutes later.

For his coolness and bravery Capt Biggs was awarded the George Medal.

* * * * * * * * * * * *

Also on 1st November, a bomb fell in the river Tyne close to the bridge at East Linton, which carried the main road over the river. Capt W M (Bill) Hewitt of 56 B D Section, No 11 B D Company, dived several times into the river, which was in flood at the time, to locate the bomb. Whilst he was not able to identify the fuze, because of the muddy water, he attempted to immunise the fuze - unsuccessfully - Finally, he returned to the bomb with a rope and with the help of Cpl Ramsey and Sapper Smith they were able to tie it round the bomb. All the men of the section joined in to pull the bomb out of the river. Lieut Hewitt was then able to identify the fuze and immunize it. The bomb was then sterilized. It was thanks to him and two of his men, in extremely cold muddy water that the bomb was prevented from destroying a very important bridge. For his bravery he was awarded the George Medal.

* * * * * * * * * * * *

By November, Lieut J P (John) Walton of No 22 B D Company, based at Colchester, had already dealt with over one hundred bombs, even dealing with them before the raid was over !

On 5th November, he dealt with four Category 'A' bombs within twenty four hours. Two were in a gasworks and it was necessary to enter a gasholder to deal with another. It was a 250kg with both a (17) and a (50) fuze. It was rendered safe under air conditions so bad that work could only be carried out in twenty minute shifts. This hazardous work, carried out whilst the raid continued, with the possible consequences from the gas, ensured the minimum damage to the gasworks and allowed services to be resumed in the shortest possible time.

* * * * * * * * * * * *

On 6th November 1940, 2/Lieut J (James) Barnes of No 4 B D Company was called to the factory of Vauxhall Motors, Luton, where ten bombs had fallen during the night. Whilst the damage appeared to be superficial, there were two unexploded bombs on the site.

One of the bombs had fallen in the Heat Treatment Dept and lay alongside a continuous heat treatment furnace, which performed a vital service in the firm's production capacity. Had it exploded, it would have wrecked the Dept and put it out of action for at least ten days.

As the position was so serious, Lieut Barnes decided upon immediate action. He was successful in his efforts and removed a very serious danger of a factory shut down.

Two other bombs in the raid, which had occurred just two and a half hours earlier, had damaged a large A.R.P. control centre, with the second unexploded one nearby, which would do further damage to the centre, possibly resulting in a temporary layoff of the 9,000 workforce.

Without hesitation, Lieut Barnes personally excavated the bomb and removed the fuze before it could explode.

It was due to his cool and courageous action that this company, engaged on important war production, was fully working by the morning of the following day, with practically no time lost, except for one building only.

Lieut Barnes was awarded the George medal for his heroism.

* * * * * * * * * * * *

On 9th November a German plane crashed in Bromley, trapping a number of people in their houses. Rescue work was held up due to the fear of delayed action UXB's in the area, thrown out of the aircraft. (Bombs in or near crashed aircraft was not an Army responsibility, but an RAF one.) In spite of this Capt C W (Charles) Lea was called in to assist, arriving at 22.45hrs. In all 30 bombs were found, some buried in the debris and others in the aircraft itself. An additional hazard was that the whole area was covered in the aircraft's fuel. By skilful and courageous work Capt Lea had managed to recover and make safe all the bombs by early morning, thus allowing the rescue teams to resume their work. For this and an earlier episode involving a parachute mine in the September, Capt Lea was awarded the George Medal

* * * * * * * * * * * *

Also on 9th November, L/Cpl E W Suttle, who was in charge of a working party, went with his Section Officer to the Aeroplane Assembly Shop of the Humber Hillman factory, where there were two reported 250kg UXB's. They were about 70 yards apart and, during the morning one exploded, killing two of the working party. In spite of this, L/Cpl Suttle continued to work on 'his' bomb. At 15.00hrs that day, the bomb was identified as a 1000kg, and the fuze was immunised and the bomb made safe for removal.

* * * * * * * * * * * *

Lieut M A (Michael) Clinton of No 22 B D Company, based at Colchester, had the job of immunising and removing a 250kg bomb in Romford. Unfortunately, the fuze pocket was damaged and he was unable to remove the (17) fuze, which it contained. As the risk of explosion in situ could not be accepted, he decided to move the bomb. Whilst it was being lifted out of the shaft, the fuze began ticking. Fortunately, it stopped, but there was no knowing if it would restart and for how long it would tick before exploding.

The bomb was loaded on a truck and with great courage he decided to drive it, and the bomb to an area where it could be exploded without causing material damage. He was fortunate enough to do so, before the bomb exploded.

* * * * * * * * * * * *

Lieut R H (Ralph) Lee, of No 9 B D Company, was called to a factory where a bomb had come to rest under the machine shop in a factory on vital aircraft production work. After digging down for 45 hours, it was found to be a 250kg with a (17) fuze which was ticking. He ordered all the men to a safe distance and started work on removing the fuze. After 15 minutes he was no further forward. He got a crowbar and managed to lever the electrical part of the fuze out, but the clock remained inside and still ticking. Necessity being the mother of invention, he thought that if he filled the fuze pocket with water, it might stop the clock - (He must have gone swimming with his wrist watch on at some time !) - To ensure success he filled the shaft with water until it covered the bomb. It proved successful enough for the bomb to be removed on the following morning. Lieut Lee had spent at least 35 minutes, alone with a bomb which could have exploded at any minute. - There are not many worse situations than that - He was awarded the George Medal.

* * * * * * * * * * * *

On 16th November, Lieut C N (Neviile) Newitt, mentioned earlier for his lucky escapes in the previous two months, went to a reported UXB in Shaftesbury Avenue, which had only dropped the night before. Judging the hole of entry, it appeared to be either a 500kg or 1000kg. It had passed through a cable duct, fortunately without damaging the cable. It was given a Category 'A' and work started immediately. The bomb was recovered two days later at a depth of 18 feet and proved to be a 1000kg, which was fitted with a fuze cap, so that the fuze could not be identified. Lieut Hewitt carried out the hazardous job of removing the fuze cap. Having done so, he was able to identify the fuze. For security reasons, it was decided to steam out the TNT before removing the bomb. This was carried out successfully.

Shortly after, he was dealing with another Category 'A', at 106 Chesterton Road in Kensington. The bomb was a 250kg with both a (17) and (50) fuze. The bomb was so badly damaged that it was impossible to remove the fuzes or the filler cap, neither could the Trepanner be fitted. So Lieut Hewitt cut a hole in the bomb by hand and the bomb was steamed out. The whole of this operation was fraught with danger as a slight jar of the bomb could either have started the clock ticking or operated the (50) fuze, which would have exploded the bomb.

Needless to say, Lieut Hewitt was awarded the George Medal. Some say he deserved a higher award.

* * * * * * * * * * * *

Also on 16th November, Sgt G A Wardrope, previously mentioned, found himself at 02.05 hrs working on a reported UXB in the General Post Office, at Mount Pleasant, which had a category 'A' rating. Under such circumstances, one would expect the bomb to explode within 80 hours. TEN days later, they were still digging down to the bomb, which was eventually, found at 80 feet. It turned out to be a 1800kg bomb (Called Satan) the largest in the German range of General Purpose bombs.

For this incident and the one reported earlier Sgt Wardrope was awarded the George Medal.

* * * * * * * * * * * *

A 250kg bomb fell on the night of 19th November and came to rest by the condensers of the Nechells Gas works, in Birmingham. The report was not received by 9 B D Company HQ until 06.30hrs. L/Sgt Andrew Sanders was sent out in charge of a working party. He had, previously, dealt with five Category 'A' bombs in the Birmingham area and had been injured twice. He and his section were successful in reaching and immunising the bomb by 12.30 hrs that day.

* * * * * * * * * * * *

Also on 19th, in Birmingham a bomb was found to be lodged in the foundations of a house in Delebran Road, Sparkbrook. So unstable was the ground that 'underpinning' of the building was found to be necessary. At a depth of 14 feet, during the excavation, water burst through a cast iron main, causing the timber shafting to give way. One man was trapped in the shaft and the 'underpinning' commenced to fall away. Sgt Sanders ordered all the men off site and, securing himself with a rope, descended into the damaged shaft towards the trapped man. Fortunately, he was able to extricate the man and bring him to the surface. Without a doubt, his prompt action, regardless of his own life, saved the man's life. The whole shaft collapsed soon after.

* * * * * * * * * * * *

On 20th and 28th November Sgt Sanders was in charge of two bombs, both 250kg, in the BSA factory, where guns were being made, and in the GEC Works. His section took just four and a half hours and three hours, respectively, to dig down and render the bombs safe. For these incidents, he was awarded the George Medal.

* * * * * * * * * * * *

A 'C' type parachute mine, complete with it's parachute.

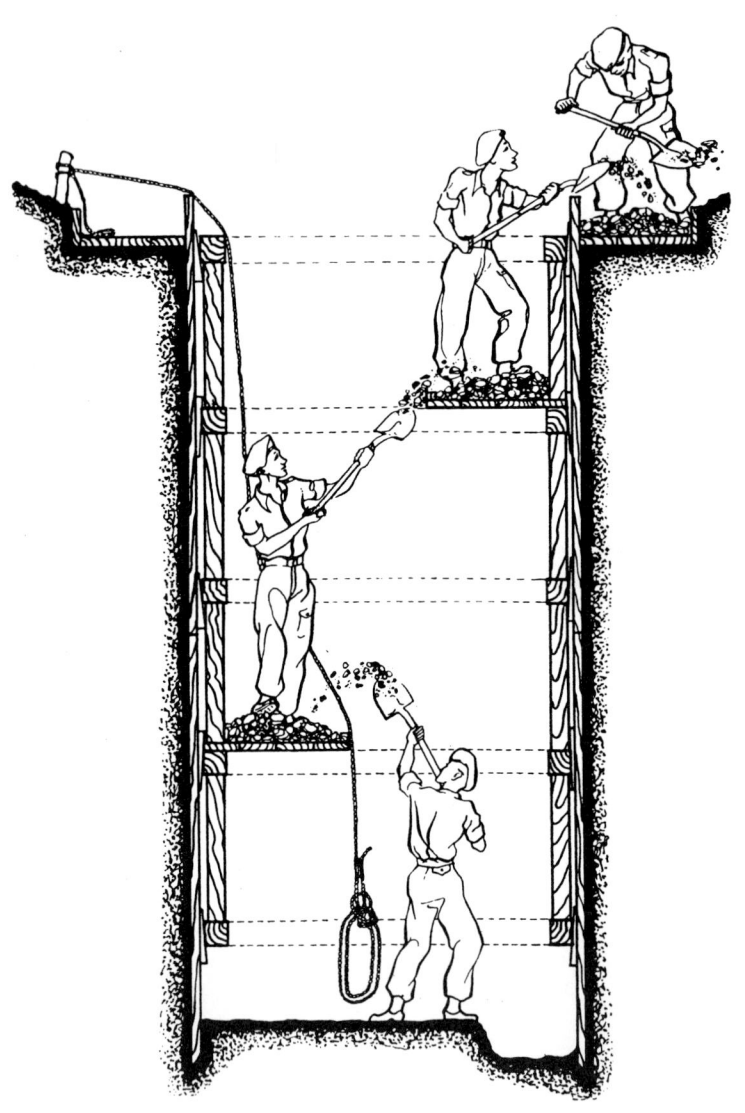

Diagram to show the method of moving soil from the point of digging to the surface. The deeper the shaft, the more men required to move the soil, thus risking the lives of more men, the deeper one dug.

Chapter Seven

DECEMBER 1940

On 3rd December, at 22.45 hrs, in Stoke Road, Slough, four bombs fell, which failed to explode. Two were given Category 'B' and the other two 'C'. One of the two category 'B's was dealt with by Capt D A (Donald) Wilkinson within half an hour of the report being received. Work on the other three commenced three days later. One of the Category 'C' was located at 12 feet and it was decided to detonate in situ, which was done without much damage to the locality. The other Category 'C' bomb was found at 12 feet and was armed with a (17) fuze. At 17.50 hrs on 5th December it was decided to leave the bomb to be dealt with on the following day as it was getting too dark to work. Within ten minutes of the squad leaving and as Capt Wilkinson was standing some 50 yards from the bomb, giving instructions on the security for the night, the bomb exploded.

The remaining category 'B' bomb was found at a depth of 12 feet and was armed with a (17) fuze. The locking ring was damaged and could not be unscrewed. It was then discovered that the fuze was ticking. The Police were warned and the streets were cleared to allow a truck with the bomb on board to be driven to Windsor Great Park, where he and Sgt Fletcher unloaded the bomb in an old crater. Shortly after, before they had left the site, the bomb exploded.

On the same night, 3rd December, at about the same time, a number of 250kg bombs fell on Eton. One went off immediately, destroying the house of Dr Ley. Another entered the roof of the Upper School passing through the building and coming to rest under the foundations of the Colonnade. Because of the damage caused, it was thought that the bomb had exploded. Although Capt Wilkinson was told the bomb had exploded, he still went to the College and was able to locate it. He then told the Headmaster (Dr Elliott) that it had not gone off. He was then requested to remove it immediately. Capt Wilkinson explained to the Headmaster that the job would take at least three days. The building would have to be shored up and that, in any case, the bomb could explode at any time. The Headmaster then offered the services of some of the senior boys, who had volunteered to help. This offer was declined and Dr Elliott was advised to evacuate the buildings for at least four days. Traffic on the Windsor/Eton/Slough road was diverted through Datchett.

The bomb exploded on the evening of 4th December.

* * * * * * * * * * * *

On the night of 9th December, a bomb fell in Sicilian Avenue, Holborn. It was inspected early the following morning by Capt W A (William) Dixon (who had already been awarded the Military Cross, before joining B D.) He found that the bomb had only just penetrated the pavement and was lying in a partly broken position near the surface.

Owing to the serious dislocation of traffic which it was causing, he decided to deal with it at once, in spite of the risks involved, which were considerable, as it was fitted with a ticking (17) fuze.

It was impossible to stop the clock owing to the distortion of the bomb, caused by the impact. The high explosive was removed from the bomb, whilst the fuze continued to tick and the operation was successful.

This was but one of over 100 bombs dealt with by Capt Dixon, including four category 'A's.

Capt Dixon was awarded the George Medal.

* * * * * * * * * * * *

On the same day, Capt D A Wilkinson was at Wargrave, recceing a suspected 250kg UXB. His section started work on 10th and when uncovered, the bomb proved to be armed with a (17) fuze. It was decided to blow it in situ and he prepared a charge, descended into the shaft, placed the charge, climbed out and had just reached the 'safe point' 50 yards away, when the bomb exploded on its own volition. Fortunately, being at that distance he was uninjured. For these two and other earlier incidents Capt Wilkinson was awarded the George Medal.

* * * * * * * * * * * *

Captain M F Blaney was a District Officer, attached to the CRE Bomb Disposal in London. The work he performed along with many acts of heroism to his credit is a continual story of gallantry and devotion to duty. He was the finest type of Bomb Disposal officer, combining the highest personal courage with the greatest possible regard for the safety of others.

He was responsible for the adoption of the policy of removing bombs whenever practicable in preference to blowing them *in situ*, thus saving hundreds of people anxiety and the loss of valuable property.

On 8th December 1940 a UXB was reported in the premises immediately abutting the main London - Chelmsford Road in Manor Park. On 13th December, in view of the serious dislocation of traffic, Capt Blaney decided to attempt removing the long delay fuze. He took this decision at great personal risk and with knowledge of the danger. Tragically, the bomb exploded and he was killed. He was awarded the George Cross posthumously.

* * * * * * * * * * * *

On 12th December Captain T H (Tom) Sharman received a call at 01.30 hrs, that there was a UXB in the B.S.A. (Guns) works at Small Heath, Birmingham. He immediately set off with his section, only to find he had been given the wrong location. After much searching he found the bomb at the B.S.A. (Tools) factory, some two miles away ! However, having got there, work was started by 03.00 hrs and and continued until 14.00 hrs on 14th when the bomb was reached with the fuze being identified as a (17), it was successfully withdrawn and the bomb made safe. During the time they were working on the bomb there had been a heavy raid, with many bombs falling close by.

* * * * * * * * * * * *

CSM Francis Smith, of 14 B D Company, spent the days of 13th to 16th December, dashing around with his few men carrying out reconnaissances on reported UXB's. Each night brought a heavy raid and additional work, but during that time he and his men were able to uncover and render safe six 250 kg bombs, all of which were fitted with (17) long delay fuzes. One of the bombs was partly buried beside large petrol storage tanks. His prompt action no doubt prevented a huge conflagration. For this and an earlier episode, in Sunderland, he was awarded the George Medal.

* * * * * * * * * * * *

On 16th, at Birmingham L/Cpl Suttle, already mentioned twice before, was working on a suspected UXB at Outlen Boulevard, when a camouflet was encountered. One man fell into the crater and was immediately overcome by the fumes. Without any thought for himself, L/Cpl Suttle immediately fastened a rope around himself and jumped into the crater, which was full of the deadly gas, carbon monoxide. He tied a second rope around the man in the crater, who was immediately pulled out. He and the sapper suffered from carbon monoxide poisoning but both, fortunately, recovered. For this incident and the two previously reported incidents, L/Cpl Suttle was awarded the George Medal.

* * * * * * * * * * * *

A bomb which fell at Aborfield on 17/18th December was started upon by Capt D A Wilkinson on 19th. The bomb was found to be a 1000kg fitted with a (15) fuze. He was told by Major H Mitchell that it was to be removed intact, apart from the fuze being withdrawn. All attempts to remove the fuze failed, so it was decided to remove the bomb as it was. The necessary lifting gear was erected and a strong cable attached to the bomb, the other end being hooked on to the back of an Albion truck 150 yards away. Capt Wilkinson was 60 yards away from the shaft when the driver mistook his signal and drove forward, jerking the bomb which then exploded. Capt Wilkinson was blown about 40 yards but suffered no injury.

* * * * * * * * * * * *

It will be seen that by the end of the year the new Bomb Disposal organisation was beginning to overcome its inheritance, which had been badly misunderstood and almost fatally underestimated. It was the energy and devotion to duty of those in the Bomb Disposal units of the Royal Engineers made possible from the morale of those involved, which seemed to evolve from the very nature of the job.

* * * * * * * * * * * *

Bomb Disposal Officers, particularly those who were in London, were fortunate enough to be made honorary members of the Royal Automobile Club. So, apart from visiting Clubs such as the Embassy or '400' Club or Kempenski's, in the Piccadilly area, the latter being considered the 'unofficial' HQ for B D Officers, we could also have a swim or a Turkish bath, before enjoying a meal at the RAC.

* * * * * * * * * * * *

On 28th, Lt W L Andrews reconnoitred a bomb at Tulse Hill Railway station and confirmed its presence. All rail traffic was stopped. On the following day he met the Divisional Engineer, who was advised that if the bomb was sandbagged, goods trains could run, albeit at a slow speed. This to remain in force until the bomb could be removed.

On 31st he exploded a 250kg bomb which was found at a depth of 14 feet, between two surface air raid shelters. Later in the day he exploded a 50kg bomb in a similar position. No damage was caused to the shelters on either occasion.

* * * * * * * * * * * *

One indication of the speed with which the Bomb Disposal units were formed and became operational is the number of bombs dealt with in the early days.

In June of 1940 some 20 bombs had been recovered and made safe. In the July it had risen to 100 and to 300 in August.

But in the 20 days from 1st to 20th September some 2,000 had been dealt with, although nearly 4,000 still remained to be dealt with.

Between then and 5th July 1941, a matter of 287 days, a record 24,108 bombs had been made safe. By then the backlog had been cleared and bombs were dealt with almost as they fell, allowing for the 'safe' period. In fact, between July 1941 and February 1945 a further 9,182 were recovered. (All U.K. figures.)

The recorded total of bombs dealt with between June 1940 and February 1945 was 35,710. In addition, some 5,673 S.D.2. Anti personnel Bombs (Butterfly Bombs) were made safe.

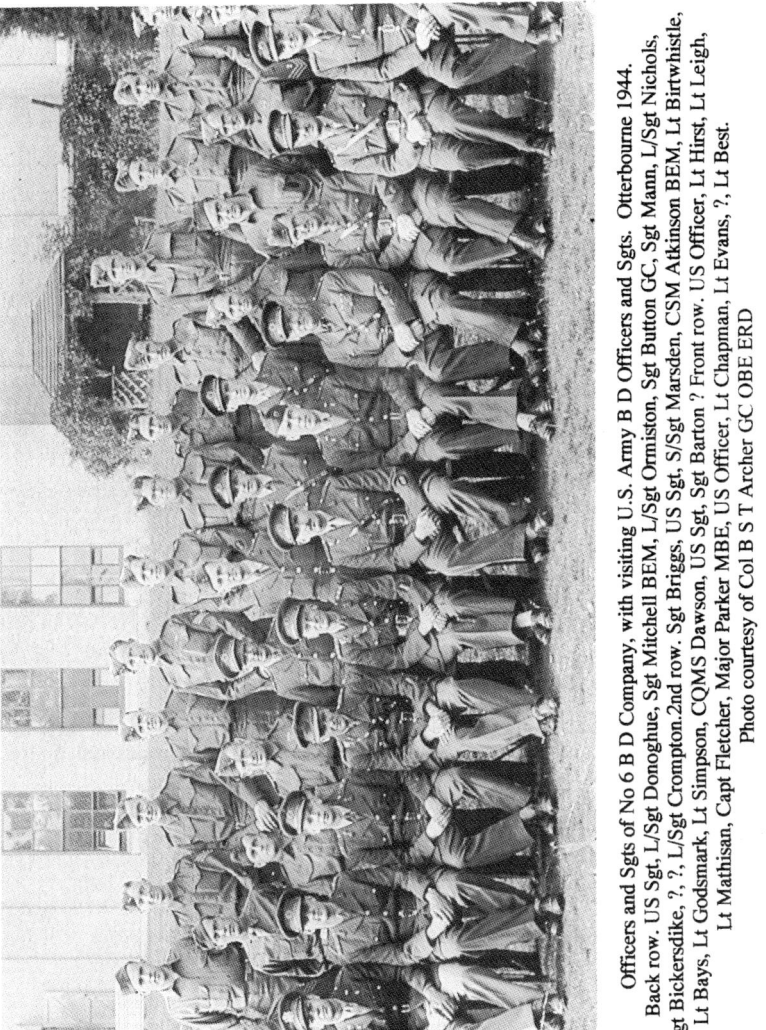

Officers and Sgts of No 6 B D Company, with visiting U.S. Army B D Officers and Sgts. Otterbourne 1944.
Back row. US Sgt, L/Sgt Donoghue, Sgt Mitchell BEM, L/Sgt Ormiston, Sgt Button GC, Sgt Mann, L/Sgt Nichols,
Sgt Bickersdike, ?, ?, L/Sgt Crompton.2nd row. Sgt Briggs, US Sgt, S/Sgt Marsden, CSM Atkinson BEM, Lt Birtwhistle,
Lt Bays, Lt Godsmark, Lt Simpson, CQMS Dawson, US Sgt, Sgt Barton ? Front row. US Officer, Lt Hirst, Lt Leigh,
Lt Mathisan, Capt Fletcher, Major Parker MBE, US Officer, Lt Chapman, Lt Evans, ?, Lt Best.
Photo courtesy of Col B S T Archer GC OBE ERD

79

An exhibit of German bombs, set up in the gymnasium of Ripon Barracks, showing recently recovered bombs. Left to Right, 250kg, both whole and sectionalised, 500kg and, extreme Right a 1000kg. Foreground 50kg's.

Photo Courtesy of Mrs S Brown.

Chapter Eight

JANUARY TO JUNE 1941

By January, the B D Companies were all 'up and running' and it was decided to return the General Construction and Tunnelling Companies back to their normal role. - To the great relief of many, but not all - No 718 G C Company left North Kent and moved to Preston. They had acquitted themselves extremely well, suffering only two injuries and some four officers and one O.R. receiving decorations. Lieut C H (Cliff) Green, who had been awarded a yet to be received, well earned George Medal, was soon sent on detachment to a Holiday Camp at Heysham, near Morecambe, to erect Nissen huts for an Infantry OCTU. He tells of their earlier problems; *"Our vehicles had not been repainted and so they still sported the red wings and the BDS badge. Our drivers took great delight in driving along the promenade shouting rude words at the 'Brylcreem Boys' of the Royal Air Force. It also had its disadvantages, in that I was approached by a local farmer, to remove a bomb from his field as he wanted to plough it. Not being in B D, I was not allowed to touch it, but I told him I would get it sorted. For at least two weeks he kept pestering me. In the end, I gave in and took a squad with me to the field. It was only a few feet down and fitted with a simple fuze,, so we dealt with it quite quickly. We took it back to the camp and burnt out the explosive, cleaned and polished the bomb and had it placed outside the Section Office.*

About a month later a young Sapper Officer arrived enquiring about our bomb. His Company had just got around to dealing with it ! Apparently it was his first bomb and the Sgt took great delight in telling him just how many we had dealt with over the past four or five months.

I decided that building Nissen Huts was not to my liking and I volunteered to return to Bomb Disposal. Major Henry was very understanding and I was soon on my way to Nottingham, to join No 3 B D Company".

* * * * * * * * * * * *

On 1st January, Lt W L Andrews was called out to a reported UXB at Marshall's Garage, Hercules Road, just by the main line running into Waterloo station. He arranged with the stationmaster for a line of coal trucks to be drawn up on the line nearest the bomb, to protect passing trains from the blast, should it explode, before it could be dealt with.

* * * * * * * * * * * *

It was at the beginning of the year that the Germans directed their energies away from London and other main cities of England to Ports and Harbours. This gave the Bomb Disposal Companies in these areas some respite, although they still had a lot of 'clearing up' to do. It was now the turn of the Companies which had coastal towns in their 'patch'. The following shows just what those coastal towns suffered.

* * * * * * * * * * * *

Lieut B H P (Brompton) Price joined No 7 B D Company, at Plymouth, in October 1940. On January 15th 1941 he went to a reported 250kg or 500kg bomb in a silo of the National Smelting works. To uncover the bomb required excavating through 100 feet of phosphate. When the bomb was reached it turned out to be a 1000kg, with a (28) fuze. It required the removal of part of the structure of the silo before the bomb could be extracted. The works were back in full operation within 12 hours of the bomb falling.

* * * * * * * * * * * *

Lieut T J Deane was with No 22 B D Company, based at Colchester. By the time he went to a reported UXB in Great Baddow, in January, he had been a 'Bomb Disposer' for six or seven months,, by which time he had dealt with around one hundred bombs.

At this reported incident, were two 1000kg bombs. Whilst his squad was 'steaming out' one of the bombs, i.e., applying steam at high pressure to melt the high explosive, thus making the bomb less of a menace, there was a small explosion and the 'fuze extension cap' blew off. In spite of not knowing what caused the explosion he continued with the steaming out. This was to be a frequent occurrence with 1000kg bombs, with extension caps, as will be seen later.

* * * * * * * * * * * *

In a raid on London on 28th January, the Streatham factory of P B Cow received two bombs, both of which failed to explode. Lt W L Andrews took his section along to deal with them. The management of the firm were so impressed with the efficiency of the Section and the speed with which they dealt with the bombs, that they were all presented with LI-LO's. (In prewar days they were 'blow up' sun beds. - They were much more comfortable to sleep on than the Army issue beds !)

Whilst they were working on these bombs, the Civil Defence were busy rescuing people from a demolished 'Old People's Home', close to the factory. On the final count, one old lady, of 90 ! was found to be missing. Amongst the debris they found an Anderson Shelter in the garden and there inside was this lady, reading a paper by the light of a candle. On being interrupted she enquired what all the noise was about outside !

* * * * * * * * * * * *

Lieut H C (Babe) Ruth, of No 14 B D Company went to deal with a Category 'A' bomb in Bridlington Railway station. He arrived at 10.00hrs and digging commenced at 11.00 hrs. Once the 250kg bomb had been uncovered and the fuzes identified as being a (17) and (50), they were immunised and the bomb rendered safe. The station was fully operational by 18.00hrs that day.

On 27th March he had to deal with another Category 'A' bomb, in Quibling's Yard, Hull. Again, a 250kg bomb with two ticking (17) fuzes. The bomb was removed from the site as soon as it was uncovered and taken to the Bomb Cemetery, where it exploded shortly after. Sgt G H Quarendon worked with Lieut Ruth throughout this operation.

Later, in May of that year, Sgt Quarendon was in charge of a section digging for a 250kg bomb in a house. It was found four feet down, under the floor, with a (17) and a (50) fuze. The (17) was ticking. On his own initiative, there being no officer present, he immunised the (50), put the Clockstopper on the (17), removed it onto a lorry and took it to the Bomb Cemetery. His quick thinking saved a nearby bakery from being demolished. A day later he was tunnelling in the debris of a bombed house, during a particularly heavy raid. His efforts contributed to the recovery of five people who had been trapped in the house. For these examples of bravery and two other incidents, later in the year, he was awarded the George Medal.

* * * * * * * * * * * *

As has already been written, Lieut F H (Frank) Butler of No 11 B D Company, which was based in Edinburgh, was 'Loaned' to No 6 B D Company, based at Reading, but he was actually sent to Southampton.

On his return to Glasgow, to his section (No 92) he continued to be extremely busy. Between 13th March and 6th May, he had disposed of 159 bombs - of various sorts !

On 13th March he went to Turners Asbestos Works to check up on a number of reported UXBs - Two of them exploded before he got there !

On the night of 7/8th May a number of UXBs were reported in the I.C.I. factory at Ardeer. Two of the UXBs had been given Category 'A.1' as they had fallen in the 'Black Powder' section of the factory. When they started work they found extremely difficult conditions in that the soil they were digging was affected by the tidal waters and running sand. In spite of all their problems, they managed to reach it, at 15 feet, and immunise the bomb in just 120 hours, thus allowing production to restart.

The second bomb was just outside the 'Black Powder' building. Work on this was then started. Similar conditions prevailed, but they persevered and at 16 feet running water hampered their efforts. The tidal waters were having a great effect on the conditions in the shaft they had dug. They gave up, and started a second shaft, this time with sheet steel piling. Even then, each time the tide came in the water 'boiled up' from under the piles. At 18 feet they recovered the tail fins, but not the bomb. A THIRD shaft was then dug. Which was taken down to 20 feet where they found a 1000kg bomb, with a (38) fuze. The date was 13th June - three months hard work !

A third bomb on the I.C.I. site was a 250kg and had penetrated to 14 feet. This had the usual combination of a (17) and a (50) fuze. In this case, the explosive was removed by steam, which took 42 hours.

The whole of the plant was back in production. It must be remembered, of course, that if any one of the three bombs had exploded, the whole Black Powder Magazine would have erupted, causing extensive and widespread damage over the area

* * * * * * * * * * * *

Lieut J P (John) Walton, who has already been mentioned earlier, had another problem on 12th March at Purfleet. The Tunnel Cement works, to be precise.

A 250kg bomb had fallen, coming to rest close to a 3,000 volt transformer and switchgear. It took 12 hours to dig down through 12 feet of chalk - some hard going ! - In addition to the difficulty of digging chalk, there was an influx of water into the shaft and there was never less than 12 inches of water at the bottom of the shaft.

When, eventually, the bomb was uncovered it was found to have a ticking (17) combined with a (50) in the other fuze pocket. The situation was further complicated by a sudden inrush of water into the shaft which made it impossible to immunise the fuzes, so a decision was taken to move the bomb ! The move was successfully achieved and the fuzes were removed. The (17) detonated about ten hours after it had been extracted.

Major General G S O Taylor, The Director of Bomb Disposal. wrote;- "*Lieut Walton has displayed deliberate and coldblooded courage of the highest order. His incident in Romford in November 1940 was a classic example, since apart from the fact that the bomb contained a combination of the most dangerous fuzes and was likely to explode at any moment, the addition risk of fire, gas explosion, asphyxiation were considerable. In addition the work was carried out whilst enemy airplanes were overhead and with ever present possibility of further hits being registered.*

Purfleet was a further example of the highest courage sustained over a long period under appalling conditions. Again, the bomb contained the most deadly combination of fuzes and may have exploded at any time during the operation. That it did explode some hours after it's removal is positive proof of the very grave dangers present during the work of its removal."

Lieut Walton was awarded the George Medal for his outstanding bravery during the two events quoted.

Cpl Bristow, who assisted Lieut Walton on these two incidents plus a further UXB in Rainham on 27th February, was also awarded the George Medal.

The bomb at Rainham was one of a stick of four 250kgs, Which had straddled the A13, one of which had exploded 18 hours after the raid. The remaining three were recovered on consecutive days, after the four day safety period had been observed. All were found to have both (17) and (50) fuzes fitted. Of these, two were found to be ticking, when uncovered. Fortunately, both bombs were successfully immunised.

Major General Taylor was also moved to comment on Cpl Bristow's courage.

* * * * * * * * * * * *

On 14th March, Lieut M A (Michael) Clinton reached and uncovered a 250kg bomb, which had two fuzes, the normal (50) but a new version of the delayed action fuze - a (17)A. This was believed to be the first of its kind to have been discovered, unexploded. He decided to remove it for research purposes.

The bomb was in an awkward position, with both fuzes being underneath the bomb. He disregarded all safety precautions and decided to remove both fuzes by hand, which he completed successfully, in torchlight.

Major General Taylor commented that Lieut Clinton had accepted the risk of certain death with sustained courage and complete disregard for his own personal safety. At this time, only a Stethoscope was available to check whether the fuze was ticking. Nothing existed to stop the clock if it was. There was also a strong possibility that there would have been a booby trap under the (17)A, to prevent it falling into our hands.

For this incident and the one at Romford in December, Lieut Clinton was awarded the George Medal.

* * * * * * * * * * * *

Lieut L (Lewis) Gerhold was another officer who had luck on his side. A bomb fell on a house in Bilbowie Road, Clydebank at 01.30 hrs on 14th March. He 'recced' it at 11.00 hrs on 15th and it exploded just three hours later. At 00.15 hrs on 8th April a bomb fell in the grounds of No 49 Polworth Gardens and failed to explode. He was there to 'recce' it, but found that it had already exploded at 10.10 hrs.

On May 7th a bomb fell in Tannochside Colliery, stopping work in the whole site. It took five days of digging to reach the bomb, which had a (17) and (50) fuzes. The (50) was immunised and the (17) 'Stopped'. The bomb was then steam sterilized by 12.00 on 12th.

Lieut Gerhold was also responsible for dealing with another bomb dropped on the night of 13/14th March at No 2 High Level Rothsay Docks which was found to have penetrated to a depth of 22 feet, where both a (17) and (17)A fuze were uncovered. Problems existed, due to tidal waters, which affected the water level in the shaft. Because of the working conditions, the bomb was not rendered safe until 3rd April. For all these incidents, and many others Lieut (Later Major) Gerhold was awarded the George Medal.

* * * * * * * * * * * *

A third Category 'A' incident dealt with by Capt T H (Tom) Sharman was on 10th April. it was also in Birmingham, at the Wolseley Motor Works in Small Heath. It proved to be a 250kg bomb with the usual combination of a (17) and a (50) fuze. Speed, of course, was always essential with Category 'A' bombs, partly because, if fitted with the usual combination, it could explode at any time up to 80 hours from the time of falling. Secondly, a Category 'A' was usually given to any bomb which was holding up vital war production, as this one was. Capt Sharman had this one removed within 14 hours of it falling.

* * * * * * * * * * * *

About the 12th April 1941, the Officer Commanding No 3 B D Company, Major J R F McCartney GM, stationed at Nottingham, was requested to send four B D Sections to No 9 B D Company at Birmingham, which had more UXB's than it could cope with.

133 & 134 B D Sections, from Derby, commanded by Lieuts Duffield and Cunliffe, respectively, and 136 & 137 B D Sections, from Melton Mowbray, commanded by Lieuts A C Thomas and Wakeford, were immediately despatched.

On 16th April, Lieut Cunliffe and his Sgt were killed, followed by Lieut Wakeford and his Sgt on 24th.

Cpl Fred Norman was in 137 B D Section at the time and describes the last moments of Lieut Wakeford and Sgt Hildreth;-

The bomb had hit a 'predictor' on an Ack Ack site, then passed through 12 inches of concrete. It had gone down about 12 feet and had veered off from the normal, expected, path. It thus needed some tunnelling to reach it. When it was reached the Lieut placed a Doctor's stethoscope on the bomb and a fuze could be heard ticking.

It was a Category 'A' bomb and so they had to continue work on it. He phoned Company Headquarters for the 'Steaming Out' equipment, but that would have taken hours to get there. He returned to the shaft with the Sgt and into the tunnel. He soon came out again and I thought he had changed his mind. Instead he took off his S D Cap and threw it up to me, telling me to look after it. I stood there, watching him return to the tunnel. The Sgt looked up at me and said "Go on, Corporal, you don't want to be here." I walked away. I had only travelled about 15 yards, when there was an almighty explosion behind me. I was blown to the ground.

Very little was found of either the officer or the Sgt.

We returned to Melton Mowbray four days later.

* * * * * * * * * * * *

It was about this time that Cpl William Hone was assisting his section officer in the factory of Morris Mechanisms Ltd, Coventry, where a 250kg had come to rest under a capstan lathe. The bomb, when it was reached proved to have (17) and (50) fuzes. A certain amount of relief was registered, when it was realised that they had been using a pneumatic drill on the concrete, before digging down to the bomb. The bomb was reached and immunised within eight hours of work commencing.

The next job was in the Daimler factory, where a 1000kg bomb had come to rest. It had penetrated 20 feet and at that depth the ground was waterlogged. The fuze could not be identified and so it was decided to steam out the explosive. The base plate (filler cap) could not be removed and so a hacksaw was used to cut it off. All this took place in very adverse conditions and took five hours.

Cpl Hone was rightly awarded the George Medal for his brave efforts.

* * * * * * * * * * * *

Sgt Thomas Taylor experienced the trauma of an incident which we all dreaded in the early days - The collapse of the shaft in which we were working. On 15th April, whilst assisting his Section Officer, Lieut Hoare, there was a partial collapse of the shaft and Lieut Hoare was completely buried. Assisted by Cpl Bardley and two Sappers, they started work on extricating their officer. Fortunately, they were quick enough to reach him before he suffocated and he was pulled out alive, but taken to hospital. Sgt Taylor continued to recover the bomb, which proved to be a 250kg fitted with both a (17) and a (17)A fuze. Lieut Hoare discharged himself from hospital to defuze the bomb. Whilst he was doing so, it exploded killing him and Cpl Bardley.

On the following day Sgt Taylor, undeterred by the previous day's accident, led two parties to a 500kg bomb and a 250kg, both of which he successfully defuzed, without further casualties. For his coolheadedness and calculated bravery, he was awarded the George Medal.

* * * * * * * * * * * *

On the nights of 21, 22, 23, 28 and 29th April, Plymouth and Devonport suffered very heavy bombing. During that time Lieut B H P Price, mentioned earlier, reconnoitred thirteen Category 'A' bombs, 147 Category 'B' and 69 in Categories 'C' and 'D'. On the night of 22/23rd he was called out to a Category 'A' bomb. Driving himself through streets almost blocked by craters and surrounded by burning and collapsed buildings, he finally reached the reported UXB, which was a 250kg with a (15) fuze, on the surface. He immediately defused it, thus avoiding the necessity of evacuating the Guildhall and preventing serious dislocation of the Civil Defence Services. For this and the earlier incident, he was awarded the George Medal.

* * * * * * * * * * * *

Sgt Thomas Williams, of No 4 B D Company was sent to a Category 'A' bomb in the Marconi factory in Chelmsford on 10th May. When the bomb was finally found, it was buried under the debris and wreckage caused by other bombs, it proved to be 500kg complete with a ticking (17) fuze.

* * * * * * * * * * * *

In May of 1941, Lieut T J Deane, already mentioned above, was called to an incident at Saxmundham. There were four 250kgs, which had fallen, that evening, in the Railway yard, Gas Works and Petrol Depot. They were all classified as 'A'. Work on all four was immediately started. Naturally, it was assumed that they would contain the usual combination of a (17) and a

(50). They were, of course, working in the 'danger period' - and in the dark !

Fortunately, as each bomb was reached, it was found to be fitted with a (25) 'Impact' fuze. This did not, of course, detract from the bravery of the officer and his men.

For this incident and the one mentioned earlier in 1940, plus a number of occasions when he assisted the Royal Navy with 35 parachute mines, he was awarded the George Medal.

* * * * * * * * * * * *

Lieut F H Butler, already mentioned earlier, went to a reported UXB in the Blackburn Aircraft Factory at Dunbarton. It turned out to be a 50kg bomb fitted with a (15) fuze.

Work commenced on 8th May, although it had only been dropped the night before. Being in an aircraft factory, it must have had a Category 'A'. It required cutting through six inches of concrete and, fortunately, only having to dig a shaft to a depth of four feet. The bomb was immunised and removed within four hours, thus enabling the factory to get back to its full production.

For his bravery during the events reported, he was awarded the George Medal.

* * * * * * * * * * * *

Four happy sappers of No 137 B D Section with the 250kg bomb which they have just recovered from the shaft which took them several days to dig.
Photo courtesy of Sgt Norman.

Lieut A C Thomas with his section (No 137) soon after their return from Birmingham, with some of the bombs they recovered during their tour of duty there. Lieut Thomas is third from the left in the front row.

Lieut A C Thomas with his section, having successfully recovered a 250kg bomb. Lieut Thomas in in the middle row, wearing a forage cap.
Photos courtesy of Sgt F Norman

94

Chapter Nine

JULY TO DECEMBER 1941

Lieut B L (Brian, known as Ricky) Richards had a very 'dodgy' bomb by anyone's standards. During the digging down to the bomb he found it necessary, on a number of occasions to stop work and withdraw his men from the shaft. Water was the problem, in gravelly ground, causing it to soften and covering the bomb. Lieut Richards insisted in doing the digging himself. The bomb was fuzed with a (17) fuze which had started ticking, only to stop. Subsequently, it began ticking intermittently. An important road junction had been closed for nine days and so it was decided to explode the bomb, should it stop ticking for any length of time. The time eventually came and Lieut Richards made up a charge. This was a dangerous and gallant thing to do as, by now the bomb was under three feet of muddy, gravelly, water. He could have got stuck in it. However, he was successful in placing the charge of the bomb and it was exploded, causing much less damage than had been expected. No doubt due to the 'tamping' effect of the water.

Lieut Richards worked, continuously, for 18 hours, never risking the lives of his men, but taking that risk himself.

General Taylor made the comment that "*Under the peculiar conditions, namely a clock that had been ticking was left for the prescribed safety period and then started ticking again, even though intermittently, it can only be said that conditions of operation were those of extreme danger. Owing to the water and the position of the bomb, after which it would automatically explode. The fact that there was so much waiting about to try and obtain safe working conditions (Which, in fact, never became possible.) was sufficient to dampen anyone's ardour, especially at night.*

I consider that this is an outstanding example of cold-blooded courage and determination for which the award of a George Cross would appear appropriate.

A George Medal was awarded

* * * * * * * * * * * * *

On 13th August, Lieut E E (Eric) Wakeling took over command of 137 Section of No 3 B D Company, then stationed at Pelham Hall just outside Gainsborough. The Section had not long returned from Birmingham under the command of Lieut A C (Tommy) Thomas, who was later to be awarded the George Medal. Most of the 'jobs' were along the River Humber, extending from Grimsby. One 'job' at Winterton had to be abandoned, because of the depth of the bomb - a 500kg - and the condition of the soil. It was recovered in 1948 by Capt P Wadsworth, reported later in the book.

The Section moved to a Vicarage in Stamford on 15th September and on 19th, ten bombs were reported at Etton. Because of pressure of work, no attempt was made to start on them until 30th, by which time two had exploded. In spite of the fact that the remaining eight could explode at any time, should there be any vibration or shock to the ground, Lieut Wakeling put two squads on the job. It took two weeks to reach and uncover the bombs and render them safe.

A bomb was reported on October 15th, a 500kg bomb at Sutton Bridge, just outside Kings Lynn - in Norfolk. They spent almost as much time travelling to and from the bomb as they did digging for it! He quotes:- *Although I didn't know it at the time, it was close to an*

96

R.A.F. station. It wasn't a Category 'A', as it did not prevent aircraft from flying, but it was a hazard.

Armed with a one inch to the mile Ordnance Survey map, we duly arrived at the map reference. Looking across the field, I could see the raised bank of the drain about 400 yards away. I thought this was going to be another 'Needle in a Haystack' job - looking for a comparatively small hole in a rather large field. - However, I saw a pole stuck in the ground some 350 yards away. Close to the post was a hole in the ground, about two feet across. It was a bit ragged and I could not be sure whether it was a 250 kg or 500 kg. With these two bombs, size didn't matter, as they were the only two in the German range which could have two fuzes. - The usual combination being a long delay and an 'anti handling fuze! The heavier one, of course, could be deeper !

The hole of entry wasn't giving my information - it had 'weathered' quite a bit since the bomb had entered the ground. I could get an approximate line and angle of entry, but when I used the probe I got absolutely nothing. Just a few feet down the ground was as soft as - Blancmange, would be a polite word for it - I could tell that we were going to have trouble with this one. It was obvious that, because of the close proximity of the drain, the water table was very close to ground level and we would need all the pumps we possessed in the section. - And the bomb could be anywhere.

At the end of the first day of working we had got down about five feet. The soil was beginning to get wet and difficult to dig. By the end of the second day we were down to the water table. Pumps would be required on the next day.

On the third day we were in deep trouble. The shaft was only about 12 feet deep. The men appeared to be shovelling thick soup. They were up to their knees in a watery looking mud and we were not making any headway. The bomb was about two feet below the surface *of the bottom of the shaft. Even though we had dug all day, we didn't seem to get any closer.*

I put on my gumboots and went down the ladder into the shaft, stepped onto the floor and felt my feet sink into the mud. It was what is sometimes called 'running sand'.

I still doubted that we would ever get down to uncovering it.

This was, obviously, a most awkward bomb. After three more days of hard work without much more progress, I decided upon drastic measures.

I stripped off to the waist and wearing just my gumboots and trousers climbed down the ladder to the bottom of the shaft, by putting my arms into the mud, I could just feel the bomb, but I knew I would never be able to identify the fuze, or even fuzes. I was now sure that it was a 500 kg bomb, which could have either one or two fuzes. So, I decided that we were wasting a lot of time and that the only way was to blow it up.

Cleaning myself up from a bucket of water, I dressed and set off for the local Police Station. On arrival I asked to see the Duty Officer. Having introduced myself, I told the Inspector that I was going to blow up the bomb on the following morning at 11.00 hrs. I then asked him to ensure that everyone was advised. That residents opened their windows to minimise the effect of blast and that they should stay clear of glass, in their homes. The Inspector assured me that everyone in the area would be advised.

We arrived early on the site on the following morning, loaded with gelignite, detonators, cable and an exploder. gelignite was a 'soft' explosive which could be moulded into whatever shape required, thus getting a close contact with the bomb. It was the forerunner of 'Plastic' explosive. If I had used guncotton, which came in 'hard' bricks, it wouldn't have been so effective.

I gave the Cpl definite instructions where to site the safe point, from which we would explode the bomb and to get the cable laid out from the safe point to the shaft. After all, it was a bomb which weighed over one thousand pounds - about half a ton. - Of which over 50 per cent was high explosive !

Dressed slightly differently from the way I was on the previous day - I now had on just bathing trunks. Not even any footwear, which would have been a waste of time for this effort. I knew I was going to get VERY muddy - all over ! (It was good thing that the weather was very mild for the time of year !) I went to the shaft, climbed down the ladder and stepped off it onto the bottom, sinking almost up to my knees in the silt. Putting my arms into the mud, I began to feel for the bomb. The whole of the front of my body was now in the mud. The bomb had moved in the night and with the whole of my arm and part of my shoulder in the muck, it was only just within my reach.

Taking four four-ounce sticks of gelignite out of my haversack, I unwrapped them and moulded them together. That would make it easier for me to make contact with the bomb. Finally, I pushed a pencil in the centre of it, to make a hole for the detonator. After a struggle, with both arms and my chin in the mud, I was able to place the explosive on the shoulder of the bomb near the baseplate and fervently hoped that it would stay where it had been placed. I then took an electrical detonator out of my haversack, reached out for the ends of the cable ends which the Cpl had lowered down the shaft. Having connected the wires, I wrapped the two joints with insulating tape, ensuring that there was sufficient cable to reach the bomb. Holding the detonator, I put both hands into the mud. With my left hand I sought to find the pencil in the explosive. Having found it, I brought my right hand with the detonator to it. By now most of my face was in the mud, I could just breath. Pulling the pencil out, I replaced it with the detonator, thus ensuring that I would not set off the detonator with the friction of pushing it into the explosive.

Making sure that all was as it should be, I climbed up the ladder, untied it and pulled it out of the shaft - No need to blow that up with the bomb - After all, I was going to lose most, if not all, of the timber !

I walked back to the safe point with the ladder on my shoulder. I checked that the sentries had been posted in a circle around the site, by the Cpl, at approximately 250 yards radius, that there was no-one in the danger area and that the remainder of the men were under cover. Then I took the exploder handle out of my haversack locked it in to exploder, pulled it up to its fullest extent. Connected the two leads, the other ends of which were now connected to the detonator.

"Everyone ready ?" I asked. The Cpl confirmed. I stood up, blew my whistle three times - the agreed signal - and said "Right, here we go then." With both hands I pushed the plunger down. There was an almighty explosion, as five hundred pounds of high explosive erupted only 250 yards away.

Looking up, I saw my precious timber (It was in those days !!) rising from the shaft soaring one hundred feet up in the air. All I'm going to get out of that lot, I thought, is matchsticks !

No sooner had the timber and mud, which had made such a spectacle, stopped falling than I heard the sound of a car approaching. It was a Service vehicle, then I noticed the R.A.F roundel on the mudguard of it. Before it had finally screeched to a halt, a very irate Squadron Leader was out and stalking towards me.

I felt a bit of a 'berk' standing there, wearing only bathing trunks and liberally covered in mud with, of course, no badges of rank on my shoulders !

"What the hell do you think you're up to ?"

Needless to say I was a little surprised and said "Disposing of a bomb."

"Well God knows what you have done to all our delicate equipment on the station." I quickly recovered my composure, in spite of the rank of the officer in blue, I said; "I advised the local police that I was blowing this bomb up at 11.00 hrs, and that's just precisely what I've done. If they didn't advise you, then don't blame me. I didn't even know you had a station near here!"

The Squadron Leader glared at me and strode off muttering something about 'Service Communications'.

I wondered if I might get a 'rocket' from my O.C. but I didn't. No doubt the Sqn Ldr had something to say to the local police. That was fortunate for me, because I hadn't told my O.C. that I was going to blow it up, instead of defusing it. (Actually, My War Diary does state that it 'Was blown in situ'!)

* * * * * * * * * * * *

Lieut H C (Babe) Ruth, who has been mentioned before, was called to a bomb incident, during a heavy raid on Hull. It had fallen just outside the Fire Station. He soon discovered that it was one of a 'stick' of four, one of which had exploded sometime after it had fallen, indicating that the others could contain delayed action fuzes. With the Fire Appliances, which were needed to fight the raging fires, still in the building, he took the risk of standing by the hole of entry and directing the vehicles safely out of the station. The bomb exploded shortly after, when he had left to visit the premises of Priestman's, where a 500kg bomb had been reported. He and Sgt Quarendon dug down to the bomb - it was only four feet into the ground - In spite of its short passage through the earth, bomb fuzes were unidentifiable, as the tops had been torn of. The bomb was immediately put on a truck and taken away. The factory was back at work by 09.30hrs, that day. For this incident and those reported previously. Lieut Ruth was awarded the George Medal.

* * * * * * * * * * * *

Lieut D L (Don) Anderson of No 19 B D Company, tells of a problem he had with a camouflet. (A camouflet is a cavity in the ground caused by a bomb exploding without breaking the surface.) A stick of 50kg bombs had fallen on the Vauxhall works at Luton. All but one had exploded and this, in a field of stubble next to the factory, looked like a camouflet. Because it was classed as 'unexploded' it affected the works and it had to be 'proved', one way or the other, as soon as possible.

"In our impatience, the earth auger (A piece of equipment designed to dig a circular hole in the ground about ten inches in diameter.) went further than was intended - right into the camouflet - and we were having difficulty withdrawing it. I didn't fancy having to dig the auger out, so I stuffed some straw down the hole we had made and lit it. The auger went twenty feet in the air, fortunately landing without any damage to person or property !

At that moment a Staff Captain appeared and inquired about our 'bang'. On the inspiration of the moment I said that the risk of augering into a camouflet in flinty soil was that a spark might explode the carbon monoxide gas and this is what appeared to have happened.

The next time I attended a B D Course, I was delighted to be warned of the possibility of an explosion when augering down to a camouflet in flinty ground."

* * * * * * * * * * * *

A typical working shaft. Note the number of 'wedges' on the staging. These are used to hold the timbers in place. Note, also, the special wooden headed, long handled mallet, used to hammer them into place. - Smoking was allowed on the job.
Photo courtesy of Sgt F Norman

A 'camouflet' under a suburban street. (A camouflet is created by a bomb which has exploded so deep underground that it hasn't the power to break the surface and make a crater. It will be in the shape of a sphere, full of deadly carbon monoxide.)

Chapter Ten

JANUARY TO JUNE 1942

Up to the end of 1941, we had been subjected to 18 months of almost continuous bombing, ten per cent of which had failed to explode on impact, for one reason or another and the organisation was still under considerable pressure. Yet, in the Oxford area, No 8 B D Company, was busily engaged on putting up Nissen huts, the construction of anti tank blocks and the like. However, this was not to last for long as the Windsor/Slough area was to come in for some heavy bombing later. They were, of course, recovering from the extremely hazardous work in South Wales, where they had previously been stationed.

In the February they had about 50 NCC (Non Combatant Corps) personnel posted in and they formed two sections (Nos 104 and 154). In spite of their earlier reputation, the NCC men performed extremely well and did a good job within the B D organisation, not only with No 8 B D Company, but within the whole B D Organisation. In fact, many 'transferred out of the NCC', providing they could stay in B D.

* * * * * * * * * * * *

On the night of 28/29th April, there was a raid on York, It was the first of the 'Baedeker' raids on our Cathedral cities. (Canterbury, Exeter, Cambridge, etc.,) The defences of these cities was almost nil, having thought to be 'Open Cities' - but not to the Germans - they were, therefore, subjected to very accurate bombing because there were little or no Ack Ack defences to deter them.

This particular raid started at 03.00hrs and lasted for just one hour. Whilst being an ecclesiastical city, it also had a very important railway marshalling yard. Incendiaries were dropped on the station and two coaches of a London express caught fire. These were detached and the remainder of the train driven away, by two soldiers who were, subsequently, decorated for their quick thinking and bravery. High explosive and incendiary bombs were liberally dropped on the rest of the city.

Reports of several category 'A' bombs were received by Major Bingham, at the Leeds Headquarters of No 14 B D Company. Major Bingham and CSM Smith departed at 08.00hrs for York. After they left, more reports flooded in and because Major Bingham could not be contacted, Lieut R Sharp left at 10.00hrs to carry out a reconnaissance of the other bomb reports, returning at 13.00hrs. Major Bingham, could still not be contacted and Lieut Sharp set out, again, at 14.00hrs. During this time at least three delayed action bombs had exploded. One just 15 minutes after Lieut Sharp had inspected it. Another delayed action bomb had killed an RAF Officer and his NCO on the York airfield.

On the next day, Capt G L Whyte, the Company 2IC and Lieut Sharp went to Scorby, some three miles east of York, where three UXB's were reported. They proved to be 500kg bombs. One had fallen into a stream, which was successfully diverted, so that it could be excavated 'in the dry' ! The second bomb had partly demolished a corner shop, with living quarters above, near Terry's chocolate factory. On first inspection it looked like the result of a small bomb exploding, but on further investigation it proved to be damage by the bomb itself. On excavation a 500kg bomb was found at five feet with a (28)B6 fuze.

In a way it was a unique raid, in that, apart from the incendiaries, nothing smaller than a 500kg bomb was dropped and it could not be proved that anything larger had been dropped.

* * * * * * * * * * * *

On Friday 1st May, Lieut Sharp was instructed to bring the 'Steam Sterilizer' to York. plus the Magnetic Clock Stopper, which would be needed on two Category 'A 2's which were being worked upon in York. He took with him Sgt Wheatley, L/Cpl Jones, Spr Firth and Spr Hobson. Work had begun on a bomb in York at 16.00hrs, under Major Bingham's control and continued throughout the night. By the time Lieut Sharp arrive they were down to 12 feet, using 'open' timbering. If the ground was sufficiently stable, then half the timbers were required which meant that the digging proceeded at a faster pace. By 20.00hrs the bomb had been uncovered - at 16 feet. - The fuzes were identified as being a (17)A and a (50). Fortunately the (17) was not ticking.

Lieut Sharp had investigated the means of access for the Steam Steriliser, which proved to be negative. It would have required driving over 25 railway lines. The only other means of access to the yard was on the far side where an unloading platform with an access to the road existed. Access, apart from on foot was effectively prevented by a ten foot high wall. The distance between the UXB and the yard on the other side of the wall was too far to allow the setting up of the Steam Sterilizer.

It was decided that the ONLY way, was to put all the equipment on a wagon, and shunt it up the line. This, in fact, was done by 21.00hrs, with the clockstopper equipment riding on the front of the shunting engine itself.

The bomb was lying approximately parallel to one side of the shaft and just outside it. A 'mini' tunnel had been dug to uncover the fuzes. When uncovered they proved to be 'on the other side' of the bomb, which made the placing of the clockstopper extremely difficult. The (50) fuze was immunised by Major Bingham, with a B D Discharger prepared by Lieut Sharp, who was left to apply the clockstopper, with the assistance of Sgt Wheatley. After the removal of more soil, they were able to place it over the fuze, but not before they had removed the carrying lug, which had prevented the clockstopper from being placed correctly. The lug had been bent by the bomb's passage through he ground and a pair of 'Stiltsons' was needed. Once the clockstopper was in place, all the men were sent to a safe distance, whilst Lieut Sharp switched it on. - There was a possibility that the shock of the magnet might JUST set of the clock, if it was about to fire, when it was stopped. However, this did not happen and the clock was now prevented from starting.

During this time, the steam sterilizer had been brought up, from the truck, placed in position about 70 yards from the bomb and 'lit up'. The next job for Lieut Sharp and Sgt Wheatley was to set up the Trepanner, so that a hole could be drilled into the bomb, to allow a steam hose to be inserted, thus melting the high explosive. This operation started at midnight and continued until 05.00hrs. During which time, they stopped the steam every 15 minutes to descend the shaft and push the hose further into the bomb. All this work was carried out with the light of three railway oil lamps and one or two torches.

Whilst all of this was going on, water continued to flow into the shaft and the one Winget pump was not man enough to extract the water, which was now mixed with the molten TNT. The eight foot length of suction hose frequently became clogged up and the steaming out process had to be stopped until the hose was cleared and the pump was able to remove the 'sludge'.

Towards the end of the operation, two things became obvious. 1, The sides of the shaft were beginning to buckle and 2. The clockstopper batteries were running low. The second was easily remedied, by sending a truck back to Company HQ for more. - they arrived at 04.00hrs. The shaft was a more serious problem. Fortunately, it did hold up for the remainder of the operation, which was far from over.

One check by Lieut Sharp showed that the steam nozzle had become clogged up with TNT and was completely ineffective. Major Bingham decided that as at least two thirds of the explosive had been steamed out it was, comparatively, safe to explode the bomb. This decision was influenced by the fact that the electrical stethoscope was found to be faulty and that they did not know whether the fuze was ticking or not. The clockstopper was also suspect and so the fuze could very well be ticking. This knowledge was not divulged to the men, who returned to the shaft to remove as much of the molten TNT as was possible.

Dawn broke at 06.00hrs and one hour later an attempt was made to explode the bomb. The immediate area was evacuated and a demolition charge was placed on the bomb. The result of the explosion of the charge was that the bomb was bent, but the contents had not detonated. There was, now, an even greater risk that the (17) fuze would be ticking. In spite of this a second charge was prepared and placed on the bomb. This was also a failure and so a third charge was made up and, this time, it was placed on the remainder of the TNT inside the bomb. The other two charges had been laid on the bomb case.

At 08.00 hrs they were successful, but with considerably more damage than they had expected. Portions of rails and sleepers were thrown into the air, one rail travelling some distance landing on the roof of a coach and coming to rest inside. Fortunately, there were no injuries and a vital goods train, due to pass through York at 08.30hrs was able to do so.

No awards were made for this incident, although Cpl Lovell, who was in charge of the digging team had his his 'record sheet' inscribed with the fact that his 'Act of Gallantry' was recognised - in Accordance with King's Regulations !

* * * * * * * * * * * *

* * * * * * * * * * * *

Lieut C V (Charles) Sadler was, at this time with No 12 B D Company, commanded by Major Hardham. The latter had developed a new piece of equipment which he wanted Lieut Sadler to use on a 250kg Phosphorous bomb, which had been uncovered in Redhill. It was designed to allow a hand drill to be used to cut a hole through the shoulder of the fuze, when water would be pumped in, to desensitise the Picric Acid pellets in the fuze pocket. He tells that; "*All went well and I climbed up out of the shaft with the fuze in my hand. The CRE and 'others' who had come to see the result of the experiment backing away. I had forgotten to remove the gaine from the fuze ! Much to their consternation. Its removal should always be the first thing one did once the fuze had been taken from the bomb.*"

* * * * * * * * * * * *

Lieut Sadler had another bomb, a 1,000kg at the top of Reigate hill. It was in firm chalk which was well drained, which enabled his team to go down to 30 feet with 'open' timbering. That meant using half the number of timbers, having a space between each the width of a plank. At no time did we take the risk of digging a shaft without any supports.

The fuze, when uncovered proved to have no markings and so Field Photography was needed. This meant a wait of a day at least. "*Whilst waiting I met a charming ATS girl from Haverfordwest - Mildred Davies. She asked to see the bomb, so I took her to the site. - I wonder what happened to her ?*'

* * * * * * * * * * * *

From April to October, Lieut Eric Wakeling was Chief Instructor of the Northern Command Bomb Reconnaissance School in Leeds and was attached to No 14 B D Company, for 'Rations and Accommodation'. He was billeted with one of the Sections in Leeds, which was commanded by a Lieut Clive Leighton. He relates;- " *We* had both been in the same 'batch' at OCTU in January 1940. He was 'Operational' and I wasn't, but that didn't stop me from going out with him on various incidents, when the opportunity arose. I remember going to York, with Clive and another officer, Lieut 'Babe' Ruth. They were working on a bomb which, on that particular day - I remember it being a Sunday - The school was not open on a Sunday, the courses ran from 14.00hrs on a Monday to 12.00hrs on a Saturday. - Between the three of us, we immunised the bomb and left the NCO and men to take it to the 'Bomb Cemetery'. We then repaired to a pub in York - All in Battle Dress, mud up to the eyebrows, as we had all been down the bottom of a 15 foot shaft. There, in our chosen hostelry, were some of the 'Staff Officers' of Northern Command - The 'Chairborn Warriors' - immaculate in their Khaki Service Dress - We were just 'scruffs' and I could feel the resentment that 'such officers' should appear, looking so scruffy. Not one of us, could have cared less. We knew that we were fighting a war. THEY we just fighting a 'Paper War'.

* * * * * * * * * * * *

Whilst Eric Wakeling was away from 3 B D Company, Lieut Paul Crothall was called out in the middle of the night to Boston where a - High Priority - unexploded bomb rested close to a main high tension pylon . He writes; "I think Boston must have the worst silt in the country. How ever they managed to build a Cathedral there, I'll never know."

On arrival, he was met by the Police who took him to the site. It didn't take him long to realise that sheet steel piling was going to be required, so he was on the phone to Company HQ, with his request.

The shaft was sited in the grounds of a market garden and they hadn't been at work for long, when the owner came over to say that Paul was urgently wanted on the phone. A long walk took him to the instrument. The caller was the Head of the Electricity Power Company and tersely wanted to know when the bomb would be removed. Paul told him that he could phone again in about two weeks time and slammed down the phone.The Company Commander, soon phoned Paul to enquire how he had upset the gentleman concerned. He was satisfied with Paul's explanation.

Every time they dug down a foot, the bomb also moved down a foot. It was between 14 and 20 feet when they finally reached it. By a remarkable coincidence, it was two weeks to the day when they recovered the bomb.

Having worked in wet clothes for two weeks, Paul finished up in Boston Hospital with Muscular Rheumatism. It was not all bad. The Police found him a nice 'billet' with a lovely Landlady and he was also given the 'Freedom' of the White Hart Hotel, which was only a few steps away.

* * * * * * * * * * * *

Early in 1942, Lieut J Hannaford of No 16 B D Company was given the job of finding and making safe any bomb which had failed to explode, following an attack on a bridge over the river Usk. He found two UXB's. One in the ground near the bridge and the other in the shallows. Unfortunately, all efforts to locate the one in the river failed and it is thought that it could still be there.

Work started on the other bomb, the tail fin being found soon after digging began. The bomb was found, at a depth of 15 feet, embedded in gravel. The river at this point is tidal and work not only suffered from rising water with every tide, but each tide moved the gravel, both inside and outside the shaft, making it extremely dangerous.

The bomb was found to have a long delay (17) fuze, but the water level precluded the use of the Magnetic Clock Stopper. It was decided to remove the fuze by remote control but, at the last moment, the Merryless Fuze Extractor jammed.

Lieut Hannaford takes up the story;- *"At this point, training and commonsense failed me and I went down the shaft to investigate. Noting that the fuze was almost out of the fuze pocket, I assumed that there was no Zus 40 fitted. I removed the extractor and eased out the fuze.*

What followed will forever be imprinted in my mind.

One moment I was ankle deep in water at the bottom of the shaft, echoing to the din of two noisy pumps. In my hand was a live shiny aluminium bomb fuze. In a split second my small world vanished together with the noise. - There was silence - I vividly remember thinking how peaceful is the end.

A lifetime seem to pass then, amazingly, from above I heard the reassuring Lancashire voice of my Sgt; "Are you alright, Sir ?"

What had happened, at the moment I held the fuze, was that the rubber hose to the compressor pump had blown off, virtually under my feet, thus vaporising the water into a thick mist. The Sgt, seeing what he thought was smoke coming from the shaft, switched off both pumps - hence the silence.

I 'came back to earth', realised where I was and what I was doing - or not doing - I had not removed the gaine from the fuze. Having done that, I was climbing the ladder out of the shaft with the fuze in my hand when there was a 'crack' and a sheet of flame sped past my face. The detonator in the fuze had fired.

* * * * * * * * * * * *

Men of No 16 B D Company, at Mt St Albans, Christchurch, Newport, (Mon)
Sadly, nearly all were killed on Beach Minefield clearance at Saundersfoot- Tenby.

Photo courtesy of Capt A F J Hannaford.

Lieut A F J Hannaford 'probing' down a hole of entry of a suspected 250kg bomb, watched by his Section Sgt, Sgt Lissemore.

Spr Barkley standing at the bottom of the shaft, by the bomb. The baseplate of the bomb can be clearly seen. The shaft is 8' 10', with 'standard' timber, which had only been issued.

Photos courtesy of Capt A F J Hannaford.

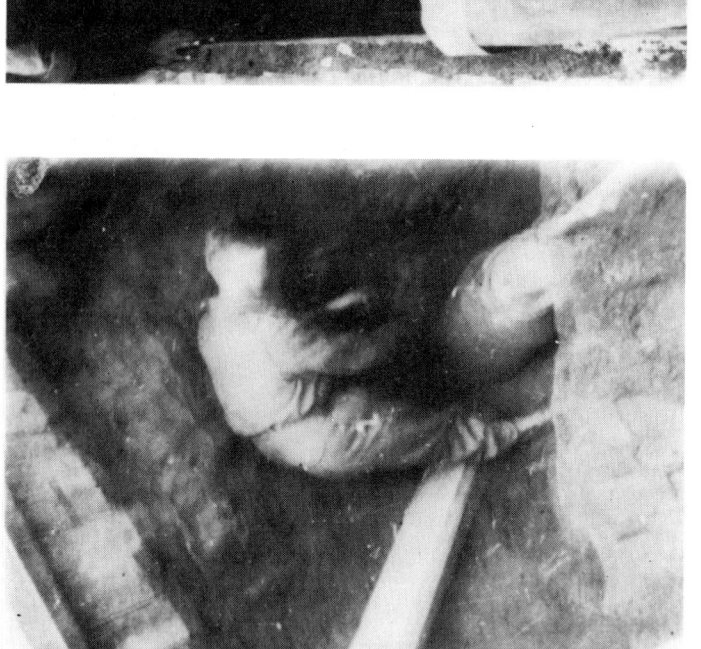

Lieut Hannaford 'immunising' the fuze of a bomb which was aimed at the entrance of the Severn Railway Tunnel.

The 250kg bomb being hauled to the surface. This method was often used if the 'Shear Legs' were not available and there was sufficient 'power' - Usually provided by a truck to pull it out.

Photos courtesy of Capt A F J Hannaford.

Chapter Eleven

JULY TO DECEMBER 1942

Even country towns, such as Melton Mowbray (perhaps the Germans were jealous of their Pork Pies) and nearby Stamford, were subject to raids. (There were, of course, a number of R.A.F. stations in the area.) Lieut Cliff Green, who has been mentioned earlier, had bombs in both towns. In Melton Mowbray, where he was stationed, he went to a reported 250kg bomb and, having dug down 15 feet without it appearing in the shaft, as he had hoped, realised that it had shot off at a tangent and he needed to tunnel some six feet to reach it, when it was found to be in a vertical position, with the nose uppermost. The clay surrounding the bomb was almost entirely removed - some had to be left to keep it immobile - but no trace of a fuze could be found. He decided that it would have to be moved out of the tunnel to find the fuze and identify it. With his Sgt, he slowly removed the rest of the clay holding the bomb and gently lowered it. As they prepared to clean the bomb down to find the fuze, there came a shout from the Sapper on 'Listening Watch'; "IT'S TICKING'.

Neither of them remember climbing the ladder. In fact they both reached the top of the shaft at the same time! Probably having climbed up the timber !

The bomb exploded about an hour later.

At another incident he found a 500kg Semi Armour Piercing bomb beside a Pumping Station for a Main Drain in the Fens. It was lying on the surface. Nearby were two holes, one where the bomb had entered the ground and the other where it had come out. Dropped, no doubt, from a low flying aircraft. The fins were found close to the surface in the the hole of departure. The bomb was a normal impact/short delay fuze and was immunised, withdrawn and the bomb taken away.

A few days later, he went to No 45, Drift Avenue, Stamford, where a UXB had been reported. It was found some ten feet down and proved to be a 500kg, with a simple impact fuze. No problem, no hassle. The only reason why this bomb is remembered is that on 18th May 1945, the local paper ran an article about the raid and included a photograph of Lieut Green and the local Police Officer involved at the time. He was sent a copy of the paper.

* * * * * * * * * * * *

Lieut C V Sadler with Sgt Hayes carrying an immunised 50kg bomb. Worthing 1942.
Photo courtesy of Capt C V Sadler.

118

Lieut C V (Charles) Sadler of 12 B D Company was at this time working in South Sussex. He and Sgt Hayes recovered a 50kg bomb. The Sgt calmly carrying it to the truck for transit to the Bomb Cemetery. A few days later he had another bomb in Worthing which reached a depth of 30 feet. The ground was waterlogged and the shaft required pumping out 24 hours a day. They had almost reached the bomb when they knocked off for the night, leaving a 'Nightwatchman' to guard the equipment. The bomb exploded at 02.00hrs. Most of the blast went straight up the shaft they had dug, but a number of houses lost their roofs and quite a few windows were broken. Fortunately, neither the Nightwatchman nor anyone else were injured.

* * * * * * * * * * * *

Lieut Sadler's next job was at Hutton Cranswick. The bomb lay in a waterlogged field with a river close by. The explosion of the bomb would have caused considerable flooding. It was necessary to lay a road in order to get the timber and equipment to the actual site. In the end sheet steel piling had to be resorted to, taking it down in three stages to 30 feet. If this was not enough, 'Dewatering' equipment was also required. This meant sinking pipes deep into the ground at regular intervals around the shaft and pumping the water out of the ground, in order to keep the shaft reasonably free of water. The job took over three weeks to complete.

* * * * * * * * * * * *

On 13th October 1940 a bomb had fallen in the cricket ground at Enfield. It was estimated to be a 250kg but work was not started, because of pressure caused by 'more important' bombs. At the time, we had a considerable 'backlog' of unexploded bombs and we had to postpone work on bombs which, if they exploded would do little damage. On 8th January, 1942, the bomb exploded. No digging down to the bomb had been started and there had been no earth shocks in the area to account for the explosion. It was not thought at the time that the

Germans had produced a fuze which would explode several months after impact - the (17) fuze had a time limit of just 80 hours.

There was another incident in Coventry, where work had started on a 250kg and part of the bomb had been uncovered, exposing a (50) fuze, which was immediately immunised. Then part of the shaft collapsed and work was stopped, the bomb exploded a few hours after. This explosion, could of course, have been caused by the shock of earth movement starting the clock of a (17) fuze.

Then on a sunny Summer day in June, without any warning, there was a great explosion at Gurney Street, in the Elephant & Castle area of London. There had been no recent raids and it was assumed that it was caused by a 'Restarted' (17). As a result of this, all reported UXB's which had been discredited or abandoned were 'Reinvestigated' !

Lieut J (Jimmy) Melrose, who was in No 25 B D Company at Eltham, tells of some of the results from the reinvestigations.

"I found an S.D. 1700kg a few feet under the road surface in a residential area. Another I found was, literally, under the back doorstep of a house. It had originally been written off as a small exploded bomb."

As a result of our various discoveries, 'Teach Ins' were organised for the Police, Civil Defence, Home Guard etc - We all did those, didn't we ? After one such talk, a Warden came up to Jimmy to ask for a better look at a piece of 'Kopfring' he had shown, then said he had got a piece 'like that' in his garden shed !! The result was yet another Herman discovered and uncovered.

Jimmy also had a 250 kg with two (17) fuzes, close to the railway line at Hither Green. He says that it had been in the ground for quite a long time, and proved the success of the 'Reinvestigation' program. Actually, it was finally found only by calling in a team operating the Bomb Locator.

His most interesting story (Technically) was that on one site he had to use 'Dewatering' equipment. Getting down to 20 feet without reaching the bomb, but that was at the limit of the installed dewatering system. So, he started a smaller shaft within the existing one, and started a SECOND Dewatering system. He found a 250kg at 30ft.

* * * * * * * * * * * *

In the July, Capt D A (David) Wilkinson had now been promoted to Major and was the O.C. of No 8 B D Company, and was ordered to Mobilize his H.Q. and one section, for a posting to the Middle East. It was then that Slough and Windsor began to receive the attention of the enemy. Wokingham was bombed, followed reports of UXB's at Wick Hill and Wing.

* * * * * * * * * * * *

About this time Lieut D L (Don) Anderson of No 19 B D Company was in Norwich and was not very happy about an order that his section was to be involved with an Eastern Command Exercise. Pleas to Higher Authority in the Bomb Disposal hierarchy, that we were 'War Office' troops and not 'Command' troops were to no avail.

"One of our number had a girl friend whose father was the Regional Telephone Engineer. We asked him where was the most devastating place for a UXB. He told us 'The pavement outside the Telephone Exchange', which would immobilize communications throughout the Region. Another friend was the Chief Warden for the area and he agreed to inform Command that there was a UXB in our selected place, so all phones would be out of service for exercise traffic.

We quickly occupied the site, lifting some paving slabs to expose the vital junction chambers. The Telephone Engineer had now raised sufficient panic to bring a Senior umpire - On a white horse ! - on site. He was persuaded to move the 'incident' round the corner and declare all of us as 'exercise casualties', in time for us to return to our billets and collect our weekend passes !

* * * * * * * * * * * * *

John Setchell was promoted Major, in September, whilst at No 53 Div Battle School, but he was allowed to complete the course, before taking over the command of No 25 B D Coy. He writes; *"On arrival, I was completely unfit. - Whoever heard of a B D Officer 'walking' around his 'patch' ? - A few days of running around with a rifle - my batman's - soon sorted that out and I finished up with the Commandant's remarks; "As an older type of officer,(I was just 29 at the time !) he gave much assistance during the course and showed keenness." What he really meant was that I introduced a heap of (to him) new trip flares, booby traps and some minor explosions on all the battles we fought and which cheered the course up a lot. We didn't kill anyone on this course, but we did have a couple wounded, but they were quite a rough lot and had had three or four killed on the previous 9 or 10 courses.*

He says that soon after he became O C 25 B D Company, he had built a .22 rifle range, behind the Officers Mess, overlooking a golf course. He asked all the Company officers, to check every possible source of tankards and pay for them out of PRI funds. (A sort of amenity fund each unit had.) Soon they were awash with tankards of all sizes.

At that time I was in the habit of going up to London, with my second in command, to visit the 'Embassy', the '400' Club and, of course, 'Kempenski's', which was considered to be the unofficial H Q for B D Officers in London. John and I had decided that we would go to Town towards the end of February. Unfortunately, on 17th of that month, we had a raid. We had one UXB reported at Well Hall station and another at Brook Hospital, very near the railway line. We decided that, for safety reasons we would have to close both lines. The following day John reminded me that we had now cut ourselves off from London, by closing the two railway lines !

I told the two section officers involved, that I would donate tankards to the section which got its bomb out first. They got their bombs out within half an hour of each other. The winners got pint tankards, with the beer to go with them and the losers got half pint tankards. John and I got our evening up in Town, but stayed so late that I had to get my driver/batman out of bed to come and collect us. Fortunately, in those days, no Military Policeman would dream of stopping a B D vehicle with red wings.

We were the only Army unit to have such a distinction. It was originally designed, so that we could be easily recognised and given priority of movement. Unfortunately, we didn't have Blue lamps to flash !

I am afraid that some of us took advantage of our position, to use our P U's for *Private* use. To ensure that we would *'Get away with it'* we usually had an empty 50kg bomb in the back, so that if ever *we were stopped* we only had to show the bomb and we were on our way.

There has been a story told that, on one occasion when there was a particularly good show on at the London Palladium, at least five P.U's, with red wings would have been found in the streets behind the theatre. - Each with a bomb in the back !

* * * * * * * * * * * *

He continues; *"In Aug/Sep 1942, I had a call from the local Regional Commissioner to say that the Royal Arsenal had a funny looking thing on the foreshore of the river Thames abutting their property and would I have a look at it. 'IT' turned out to be a parachute mine. We made it fast, so that it did not disappear with the next tide and got in touch with the Royal Navy, who were still responsible for missiles below high water mark. A Lieut Tanner R.N. arrived and duly made it safe, leaving us to deal with the 'body' ! We decided to steam out the explosive. On arrival back at the Arsenal, with the* steamer, were were asked, as usual to leave all matches, lighters, etc., at the gatehouse. Pointing out that we could not use the steamer unless we had something with which to ignite it, we were met with " I can't let you in with any matches or lighters ! " I enquired who could give me permission so to do and I was given the name of some Vice Admiral who resided at the Admiralty.

Eventually I tracked the gentleman concerned to his office and explained that I needed to take matches into the Arsenal and, what was more, I wanted to light rather a larger paraffin burner. He was intrigued with our method and went away to discuss the matter with a couple of other admirals !

Finally, armed with a large signed letter by the admiral, we returned to the Arsenal. The guard obviously thought we had written the letter ourselves and there was a lot of telephoning and visitations by senior officials before we were finally admitted, with our matches. They put a Security Guard with us, to make sure that we did not use a match anywhere other than on the foreshore. When we did, eventually, light the steamer he was watching from half a mile away, using field glasses !

* * * * * * * * * * * * *

Later in the year Major Setchell left No 25 B D Company, to take up the appointment of S.O.R.E 2. (B.D.) - Staff Officer, Royal Engineers, Grade 2, (Bomb Disposal) based at H.Q. South Eastern Command, Redhill, Surrey under the command of General Montgomery.

One weekend, getting some leave, Major Setchell caught various trains, to get him to Exeter, where his wife was living. All went well until the train approached Salisbury, where he saw the Gas Holders to the North of the railway line approaching the city of Salisbury on fire. Naturally, he assumed that it had been the subject of a 'hit and run' raid. The train pulled into the station, the locomotive was then unhooked and driven away. After a wait of 20 minutes, Major Setchell left his compartment to find the Station Master, to enquire the reason for the delay. He quotes;- *"The Station Master was in what we Devonians call 'All of a Tizzy'. Apparently a single German aircraft had managed to put a bomb in the gasholder and another into the railway line, which had failed to explode. The Station Master told him that the authorities had been informed and that a Bomb Disposal team was coming from Bristol to deal with the incident. I realised that they could not arrive for another one and a half hours. As I was keen to get home, I told him who I was and offered to inspect his UXB, to which he agreed, with some alacrity ! Using the Stations telephone, I spoke to the O.C. of the Company at Bristol, told him I would check and let him know the result, to which he agreed.*

The Station Master and I walked to the end of the platform, where he told me that the bomb was about 300 yards along the track, but he wasn't going to show me where ! I made my solitary walk along the track. Sure enough, there was the sign of something hitting the track. three or four sleepers had been damaged, but not penetrated. - The bomb had 'bounced', at a point where the railway line curved away to the right and there was a set of points leading to several sidings and an engine shed, some 200 yards away. As I approached the engine shed, I met a driver and fireman who described a bomb flying past them and pointed to a hole in the engine shed, some four feet from ground level. It appeared that, because the bomb had been dropped at such a low level, it had not been 'armed' by the time it hit the railway track and, having 'bounced' and flown some distance through the air - and the engine shed - it exploded when it hit the ground on the far side of the building.

I was able to go back to the station and confirm that there was no danger from any unexploded bomb and that the train could continue on its way.

It was confirmed, later, that it was a single German aircraft and was, in fact, shot down 25 miles away.

Just another 'Engineering job' ! Which took several months to complete.

Photo courtesy of Sgt O A Kent.

Chapter Twelve

JANUARY TO MAY 1943

During the night of 17/18th January 1943 a large calibre bomb fell in the warehouse of the Victoria Haulage Co at Battersea and, after tearing its way through roof girders, floors, machines and packing cases, came to rest, unexploded immediately beneath the bed plate of a very large lathe.

Owing to the fact that the warehouse was full of new and heavy machine tools from the USA, the Ministry of Supply applied to the Regional Headquarters for a Category 'A.1'. Which meant that the bomb should be recovered, without it exploding - AT ALL COSTS - Regardless to loss of life of Bomb Disposal personnel ! This was granted and work began on the morning of the 18th January.

During the day of 18th January another Category 'A' bomb had been uncovered and found to contain an entirely new fuze which, on examination, during the night of 18/19th was found to embody characteristics which indicated that it was to be more formidable as an anti handling and booby trap than any other type before. Fortunately, Capt Carlyle, who discovered this new fuze, was able to extract the it from the bomb. (without blowing himself up) and it was found to be proof against any known technique or equipment. On the same night Major Martin's bomb was identified as a 500kg bomb with two fuzes, but the casing was so distorted as to render their withdrawal impossible. One of the fuzes turned out to be of the new type. This necessitated shutting down the machinery of a large flour mill next door and work on the bomb was temporarily suspended.

In view of the urgent need to get the flour mill back in production and for removing the threat to the machinery, which was of the utmost importance to the war effort, it was decided to remove the filling plate of the bomb and remove the explosive filling. It was found to be cast TNT which required the application of steam to melt it. This was a formidable and risky task. However, Major Martin decided to go ahead, with the assistance of Lieut Deane.

It was considered that the risk of detonating the bomb was too great for the normal application of the steam and it was decided that the only way was to 'hand feed' the steam hose into the bomb and to scrape the softened explosive out. They were also aware that any knock or jolt would explode the bomb as this particular type of fuze was the most sensitive anti handling device that the Germans produced. The normal method could not be carried out by remote control, so the officers would have to be with the bomb during the whole procedure.

The two officers worked continuously from the afternoon of 20th to 0830 hrs the following morning, by which time they had successfully removed all the explosive from the bomb. (Some 550lbs - 250 kg) It must be remembered that the conditions under which they worked was probably like being in the 'Hot' room of a Turkish Bath. They were cramped in a confined space some 15 feet down in the ground, with steam pouring from a pipe into the bomb. Apart from handling the softened TNT they would also have been breathing in air which contained particles of the explosive and could damage their lungs.

Major Martin was awarded the George Cross for his cold-blooded courage and tenacity of purpose while Lieut R W Deans received the George Medal.

Incidentally, this was the first, and only, George Cross to be awarded for a Bomb Disposal Operation in the UK since 1940.

* * * * * * * * * * * *

Another 500kg bomb fell on the same night and came to rest about 8/10 feet under the surface in a side street adjacent to the Old Kent Road. Major Martin got down to this one on 2nd February, it also had a new type of fuze.. Fortunately, the fuze extracted by Capt Carlyle, without blowing himself up, was one of this type. It had been 'researched' and the boffins had produced a quick answer to the problems which the new fuze presented. Armed with this new equipment Major Martin was able temporarily to immunise the fuze, but when he tried to extract it, he only succeeded in breaking the top off the fuze, leaving the 'business part' still inside.

He then decided to remove the remainder of the fuze, bit by bit. This took time, cool courage and dogged perseverance under condition of great physical and mental strain over a long period.

* * * * * * * * * * * *

Major John Hudson. MBE, was one of the 'Boffins' referred to above. - He was D.A.D.B.D. (Technical). - He had just the one fuze, which Capt Carlyle had recovered, for his research. Because of this, it was not possible to carry out exhaustive research which the fuze really required. However, by 24th January he had developed an 'improvised' system, unavailable to Major Martin. He experimented on a 500kg bomb which denied the use of Albert Bridge and, coincidentally, access to the flour works. .

The process relied upon the temporary immunisation of the fuze (by freezing) thus enabling the fuze to be removed whilst it was inert.

IT WAS ANTICIPATED (AND MAJOR HUDSON KNEW THIS) THAT UNEQUAL

CONTRACTION OF THE BOMB CASING AND FUZE POCKET MIGHT RESULT IN A SUDDEN FRACTURE, THE SHOCK OF WHICH MIGHT WELL CAUSE THE FUZE TO FUNCTION, THUS EXPLODING THE BOMB.

At the end of two hours, during which time the bomb casing actually cracked, fortunately, without causing the anticipated explosion. Major Hudson estimated as a result of his laboratory tests, that the fuze was sufficiently immunised to be extracted. An attempt to extract the fuze by remote control failed, owing to the 'anti withdrawal' device and so he resorted to removing it by hand. After much effort and considerable force, he was successful. He immediately removed the gaine, thus preventing the fuze from exploding anything.

The extraction of the fuze took 23 minutes instead of the anticipated maximum of 20 minutes, which was thought to be the 'safe' period in which to work.

From more research on the second fuze a much improved method of immunisation was devised, which allowed a further eight bombs in London to be immunised and extracted safely.

Major Hudson had a George Medal added to his already awarded MBE.

* * * * * * * * * * * *

On 4th February, the immunisation of, yet another one of these fuzes, was being carried out with the new equipment. Whilst it was secret at the time, it involved the use of Liquid Oxygen. This new fuze had its own batteries and thus, would stay 'Live' for as long as the batteries produced electricity - which could be months - even years! The Boffin's answer was to 'Freeze' the fuze. Once the temperature got down to minus 27 degrees Centigrade, the batteries became inert and thus the fuze was immunised. Unfortunately, if they 'warmed up', they became 'Live' again. Unfortunately, Liquid Oxygen is very volatile and can burst into flames.

On this occasion the Liquid Oxygen did explode into flames and the officer involved was badly burned. It was, in fact, Capt Carlyle, who had successfully extracted the first of these fuzes. This was his second bomb with a 'Y' fuze .

* * * * * * * * * * * *

Early in February 1995, the Daily Mail published a a story by a Mrs Ellison, who was a child during the war, about the machine gunning of children and the bombing of a school in Catford, it was headed;- 'Slaughtered children.' It bought a response, printed in that paper on 28th Feb 1995, from a Mr Easterbrook, who wrote;- *"People might not believe Mrs Ellison's letter about the German pilots machine gunning children in a school playground, but for me if brought back terrible memories.*

I was born in Catford in 1934, and lived there throughout the war. I can well remember that fateful day in January 1943, It was dinner time and I was going home with a group of my friends.

We heard the drone of low flying aircraft coming from behind us. On looking round we saw German aircraft at roof top level. We could see the pilots and the swastikas on the tail of the aircraft. There was no air raid warning.

The pilots started machine gunning us, children in short pants with our gas masks round our shoulders; there could have been no doubt in anyone's mind as to who we were.

We had been taught that in such an emergency, to jump over the nearest wall or get under a hedge, which is what we did.

After they had passed over us we heard explosions. We did not know at the time but it was our school being bombed.

Back on the pavement were the bodies of some of my school friends. A great many children died that day; I was one of the lucky ones. One cannot and should not forget what happened for their sakes.

In 1960, I was appointed teacher at Catford Central School, the local senior school, just around the corner from where the bombed school in Sandhurst Road.

(signed) J Easterbrook.

* * * * * * * * * * * *

About the same time. I had received a letter from Major J H Setchell, telling me of a similar incident. he wrote;-*" One morning in January 1943, My 2IC, Capt John Draper and I were sitting outside my office (of No 25 B D Company) when three 'Jerry' aircraft passed over at about 300 ft. A few moments later we heard explosions. About an hour later, I received a call from the Regional Commissioner, telling me that a school had been bombed and that they needed 'Engineer advice'. I arranged for two of my sections to attend and give what assistance they could. I arrived about an hour later and was horrified at the carnage. It was about two weeks before we had cleared the area, pulling out small children, in most cases mangled beyond recognition."*

I wrote to the Daily Mail asking them to send a copy of Major Setchell's story to Mr Easterbrook, together with copies of the photos. I am delighted to say that I had a letter from Mr Easterbrook, who now lives on the Isle of Sheppey, confirming that both reports were of the same incident. It happened on 20th Jan 1943, remembered as it was his brother's birthday, that day ! He is only still alive today as he was on his way home for dinner when the bombs were dropped, just after midday.

* * * * * * * * * * * *

In his book "London at War", Philip Zeilger wrote;-
"Certainly, schools seem to have been a favoured target. In mid March twenty four planes came inland; five or six

reached London; three trains and a trolley bus were machined gunned; two schools were bombed and seriously damaged - though fortunately before the children had arrived. They were less lucky on January 20th. To allow calibration work on the gun-laying radars, the barrage balloons were not flying over South East London, permitting a Focke Wulf fighter to sneak past the defences.

First it machine gunned Cooper's Lane School at Woolwich. No one was hurt, but when the plane flew on to Sandhurst Road School in Catford, Lewisham it dropped a 1,000 lb bomb, which passed through the side of the building and penetrated the ground floor. It exploded in just over a minute, which allowed some children to scramble through the ground floor windows but offered no chance to 75 or so eating their lunch in the dining room. 38 children and six teachers were killed or died in the next few days; many more were seriously wounded. A grisly photograph showed the childrens bodies covered by tarpaulins outside the school; the authorities not unreasonably concluded that this would be damaging to morale and forbade its appearance.

* * * * * * * * * * * *

In a raid on the night of 3/4th March, 346 S.D.2's (Butterfly Bombs) were dropped in Essex. They fell in open country and were found mostly on the surface. It was necessary to remove them as quickly as possible as they were holding up the collection of the crops.

They were fitted with two new fuzes, a (70)B which was an anti handling fuze, designed to explode the bomb at the slightest touch or vibration. The other was a (67) which was a time fuze, designed to explode the bomb at any time up to half an hour after it hit the ground. Owing to faulty action, or manufacture, the fuzes frequently stopped - usually a few seconds before it was due to explode, thus turning it into an anti handling device. There was also an additional problem, as many officers were to discover, the explosion of one could set off other bombs within a 25 yard radius.

The methods developed for the disposal of these bombs was that, with a (67) fuze, because of the uncertainty of what might happen if it was moved or touched, it was to be exploded by placing a guncotton charge upon it. For the explosive to be effective, IT HAD to be in contact with the bomb. This called for a gentle touch and a steady nerve. The (70)B fuze could be exploded by moving it - from a safe distance ! - This also required a steady nerve and gentle touch in that a length of string or cord had to be threaded round the wire between the bomb and it's drogue. One sharp pull would usually set off the bomb.

This was fine when the bombs were on solid ground, but if they were hanging from bushes, wire fences or even telephone lines an officer was at considerable risk, not necessarily from his own clumsiness, but also the vagaries of the weather, or rather the wind.

When the bombs were, subsequently, found in built up areas, more problems evolved, with them being found hanging from gutters, hanging through ceilings, on beds, in attics, railway wagons, up against the door of the 'outside loo' !

The day after this particular raid Lieut Thomas Blackshaw disposed of 31 bombs at Mountnessing, all of which had (70)B fuzes. Over the next two days, he disposed of a further 64 bombs. For his sustained courage in dealing with so many bombs over such a short period, where each one constitutes a very real risk, he was awarded the George Medal.

* * * * * * * * * * * *

A further raid was made on Essex and Lieut Warner Swinson was tasked with the job of clearing Chelmsford. He and his section soon cleared the area, in which Lieut Swinson personally disposing of 40 S.D.2's. Subsequently he was directed the heathland, where he found and disposed of a further 43 bombs.

* * * * * * * * * * * *

Also, as a result of that raid, Lieut Clinton went to Stisted, on 6th March. There he found 21 S.D.2's, some of which were on the surface, but others were buried. Some to the depth of eight or ten inches. They all had (70)B fuzes and, where possible, he detonated them by attaching a string and pulling them. The earth round the buried ones had to carefully cleared to allow contact of the explosive with the bomb. A dangerous situation.

On the following day he disposed of eight at West Thurrock, all with (70)B fuzes and a further ten in an oil refinery at Thames Haven. These bombs all had (67) fuzes, three of which had to be moved from where they lay, as they were under oil pipes.

For these incidents, Lieut Clinton was awarded a George Medal. - His SECOND - The first being awarded for incidents in Dec 1940 and March 1941. He was one of two officers who were awarded the George Medal Twice, for Bomb Disposal.

* * * * * * * * * * * *

A third George Medal was awarded, as a result of this one raid, to Sgt Thomas Hall, who disposed of 32 bombs, at Mountnessing, on 5th March, followed by 32 more on the next day and 19 on 7th.

* * * * * * * * * * * *

Capt Bourne was awarded an immediate George Medal for his, unspecified, work on Butterfly bombs in the same area working with his Section Sgt, Fred Fisher, who was awarded the British Empire Medal

* * * * * * * * * * * *

Before the raid on Grimsby/Cleethorpes, mentioned later, Lieut P F (Paul) Crothall, was stationed in Cleethorpes, he and his section returning to Company HQ just 12 days before the raid. In fact, he was posted from the Company the day after his return. Whilst he was there, he was called out by the Police on two occasions. The first bomb was rather small, quite unlike anything he had ever seen before. It appeared to have a simple impact fuze so he took it out on the sands to detonate it. It went off with a surprising 'Crack' indicating a high quality TNT. - I think it broke a few windows along the sea front, he said ! It was only after some research that he discovered that it was a World War One bomb, probably dropped from a Zeppelin, which must have lodged in a chimney only to be dislodged by a raid in World War Two !

The second incident was when someone brought to the attention of the Police a package of gelignite, which was in a very unstable condition, - oozing pure nitroglycerine ! - Packing it very carefully in his P.U. (Pickup truck - Utility) - he was given a Police escort through the town, to Cleethorpe Sands, ignoring all traffic lights. Unfortunately, a 'Brasshat' was held up at one set of lights and, apparently, he phoned the War Office to enquire who the lunatic might be, who went through red traffic lights. Obviously, he was not aware that we had distinctive markings, such as red wings.

* * * * * * * * * * * *

Whilst Paul was in Cleethorpes, he had a 500kg to deal with. It had gone right through a house, whilst the occupants were still in bed, missing them by just a few feet. Needless to say, they departed in a hurry, thankful that they were still alive.

It was a fairly straightforward job and we got on with it quite quickly. However, before we had finished, I had a visit from the Police. They told me that they had had a report that we were looting the evacuated house. As I had just rendered the bomb safe, I asked the Police to bring the owner back to the house, when I would be happy to return all his valuables, which I had kept, for safe custody. He was reluctant to return, as the bomb was still there, but he did. I got him to sign, reluctantly, that all his valuables were intact.

When he had gone, I told the Police what they should do with him, but they persuaded me that he was an important VIP and they would prefer not to antagonise him.

I pointed out that to have observed our actions, he must have had a telescope or binoculars, which was an illegal possession at the time and thus he had committed an offence and I thought that it should be taken away from him. This, I believe, was done!

* * * * * * * * * * * *

GERMAN SD2 ANTI-PERSONNEL BOMB (BUTTERFLY BOMB)

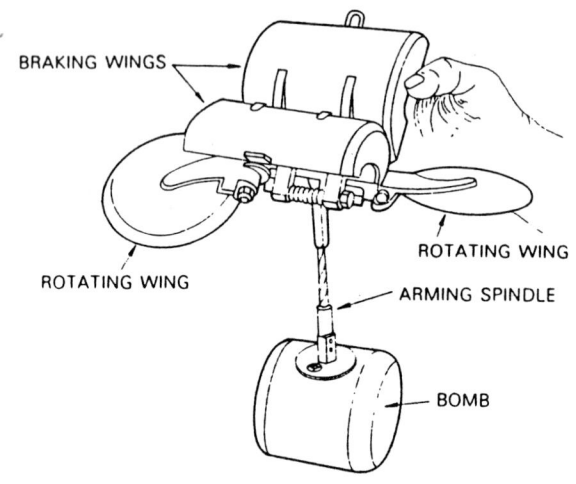

BRAKING WINGS

ROTATING WING

ROTATING WING

ARMING SPINDLE

BOMB

BOMB & CASING IN OPEN POSITION

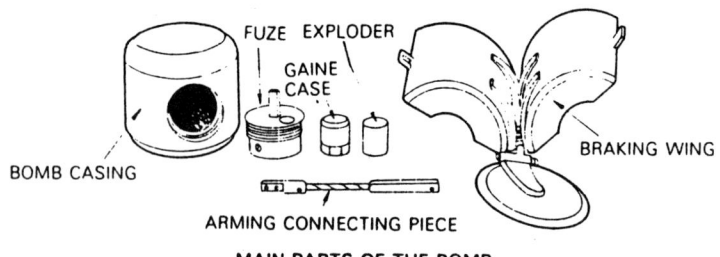

FUZE EXPLODER

GAINE

CASE

BOMB CASING

BRAKING WING

ARMING CONNECTING PIECE

MAIN PARTS OF THE BOMB

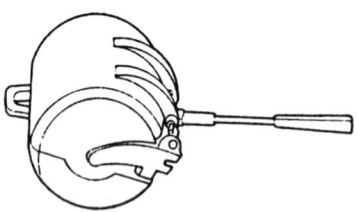

BOMB CASING IN CLOSED POSITION

138

An S D 2 - 'Butterfly Bomb'

Awkward situations in which 'Butterfly Bombs' could be found.

14∅

Chapter Thirteen

JUNE TO DECEMBER 1943

On the night of 13/14th June 1943 Grimsby suffered a most severe raid. Whilst there were some high explosive bombs and incendiaries dropped, the bulk of the aircraft dropped anti personnel bombs. Some 2,700 S.D.2's were dropped which, literarily, brought the town to a halt.

Nine officers and a similar number of Sgts of No 3 B D Company under the command of Major W G Parker moved into the area, for the 'clear up'. The bombs were everywhere. Not only in gardens, but in bedrooms and bathrooms, even hanging from ceilings. Outside they were hanging from telephone lines or power cables, hedges, fences, railway trucks, even in drains and worse, in the crops of wheat, peas, beans, cabbages, etc, which surrounded the area.

Seven George Medals were awarded for bravery in an operation which lasted less than 14 days. Four to Sgts and three to officers. There were other acts of bravery which were not recognised as the 'Powers that be' decided that they could not make an award for every act of bravery, which would have totalled about 18 in one single operation. What they, and many others, failed to realise was that in Bomb Disposal the officers and men had been fighting the enemy (In the UK) since June of 1940, every day. No other branch of the British Army had its troops in the 'Front Line', 365 days of the year as did those in Bomb Disposal. Yet, no recognition was given for their bravery.

Not even the 1939/45 Star. The following text details the citations for those awards.

* * * * * * * * * * * * *

Sgt Ashmore dealt with, amongst others, an S.D.2 which had landed under a railway wagon full of valuable goods. By means of skilful sandbagging and protective works he managed to preserve the wagon and its contents when he exploded the bomb.

He also dealt with another lying close to the signal box. It was in a very insecure position and could have moved at any time. Again, by sandbagging he was able to explode the bomb without putting the signal box out of action.

Ten days later he had to deal with one suspended by its drogues over a false ceiling. It was inaccessible from the room beneath, so having cleared the rooms of the valuable fittings and furniture, he rigged up a tackle from the chimney stack, to pull the bomb clear. After a short move of the bomb, when he tried to pull it out, it jammed and he had to return, climbing over the roof at great risk, to the bomb, freeing the tackle. When he resumed the removal, it exploded.

* * * * * * * * * * * * *

Sgt Leonard Hollands had, on 16th, a bomb in the circle of the Savoy Cinema, Victoria Street. Due to misinterpreted instructions, the ARP Wardens had completely covered it with sandbags and so it was necessary to remove some, to enable him to reach the bomb. He decided to do this by remote control, using a tackle. The friction on the tackle was too great and he entered the false roof, to pull them free from a nearer position. The bomb exploded but he escaped personal injury because of the shield the sandbags provided.

The next day he found one balanced on a gutter of Carr Lane School. In order to reach it, he climbed along the sloping roof, at considerable risk of slipping or dislodging a slate which could have exploded the bomb.

On the day after he went to four bombs on Tramway Depot Wharf, Victoria Street. The wharf was found to be constructed with old rotting and unstable sleepers. In order to minimise the possible damage to nearby buildings, he built a sandbag wall. This was extremely dangerous because of the instability of the wharf. However, he was able to do that and approach all four bombs with an explosive charge. The only damage as a result of his efforts were two broken windows.

* * * * * * * * * * * *

On 15th Lieut Gordon Jensen found a bomb resting near the base of a valuable piece of Belgian machinery in Ogle's Timber yard. The floorboards were too loose to permit the placing of sandbags, without causing movement of the bomb, which had an anti handling fuze. He attached a cord to the bomb and working on the premise that if he pulled it hard enough, it might travel a sufficient distance to prevent or reduce the amount of damage from the exploding bomb. In this he was successful and the machinery sustained minimal damage.

The next day he found a bomb under a valuable projector in the Palace Cinema. Any explosion would have caused irreparable damage to irreplaceable parts. This time, he constructed a tunnel of sandbags. By tying a cord round the bomb he was able to pull the bomb along the tunnel and out of the room before it exploded, causing five broken windows but very little other damage.

Four days later, he was on his hands and knees, trying to remove a bomb from a 'seven junction drain'. Damage to this would have caused considerable problems to a whole host of residents in the houses served by these drains. He constructed a tower of straw bales around the manhole of the drain. A magnet was suspended from the centre of the tower and lowered slowly onto the bomb. Once it had attached itself, he carefully raised it out of the drain and when it was clear, he pulled a bale of straw over the manhole so that if the bomb suddenly exploded, no damage would be caused.

* * * * * * * * * * * *

Sgt James Renfrew went to a small yard at the back of the Salvation Army Hostel, on 16th June. In a misinterpretation of instructions, the ARP wardens had completely covered it with sandbags. He carefully removed the top layer of sandbags but thought it unwise to move any sandbag which might be in contact with the bombs, so he carefully cut through a sandbag so that when the bomb was revealed he could place a charge on it. This he succeeded in doing and the bomb was detonated, causing the breakage of one small window.

On the 19th he was defuzing a bomb which, he thought, had failed to arm itself. As he was working on it, he heard it arm. He was able to withdraw the fuze and throw the bomb. Fortunately, for him, the gaine was of bakelite and had broken, thus it remained in the bomb and he suffered only from a few pieces of copper, in his hand, from the detonator in the fuze.

Two days later, he had to deal with a bomb, very insecurely resting on the pillow of a bed in No 27 Campden Crescent. In spite of this, he managed to remove all the other furniture from the room, before carrying out a controlled explosion.

* * * * * * * * * * * *

On the morning after the raid, Lieut Robert 'Bob' Sharp was one of the first officers to arrive. One of his first 'jobs' were the bombs which were holding up traffic on two railway lines as well a part of the Power Station, all had antihandling fuzes. By 16.30 hrs that day, he had personally disposed of ten bombs and restored the services to full operation.

On the next day he was wounded in the hand and leg, after having dealt with eight bombs. An undiscovered bomb exploded in sympathy with the one he had just exploded. In spite of his injuries he continued with the disposal of the bombs until the end of the day and part of the next until he was ordered by his Commanding Officer to report to hospital. He was released from hospital on 19th and on that and the following day he defused a further 32 bombs and detonated 15 others.

On 21st he disposed of 130 bombs at Calcethorpe Farm, Louth.

* * * * * * * * * * * *

Sgt Cecil Simpson personally dealt with 43 bombs, during the period of 14th - 21st June, which was the period when most of the Company's Officers and Sgts were in the Grimsby area. Typical examples of the way he dealt with them are;- On 17th he found a bomb inside the panelling of the organ in Hainton Methodist Chapel. Running the risk of exploding the bomb, he removed some of the panelling and placed a hook around the bomb. He was able, by remote control, to remove the bomb from the organ but, unfortunately, it exploded before he was able to drag it out of the church. The church suffered some minor damage, but the organ was undamaged.

On the same day, he went to 86 Fairmont Street, where he found a bomb in the downstairs front room. Like his colleagues, he removed all the furniture and fittings, before attempting to remove the bomb.

One further bomb was found on a rockery rather precariously perched so he built a wall of straw bales around it and detonated it. There was no damage to the house, although it was only five feet away.

* * * * * * * * * * * *

Lieut Alexander 'Tommy' Thomas was also there from 15th to 21st June, during which time he dealt with 73 fully armed bombs and forty six from two containers. On his second day he went to the Co-Op, stores in Freeman Street, where he found one on the floor of a room, with another hanging through the ceiling. He built a scaffold up to the ceiling and placed a demolition charge on it. The one on the floor was surrounded with sandbags. Both were detonated together and a third detonated in sympathy in the roof a short distance away.

He also found one in the false roof of Forrester & Boyd, Accountants. He tried to remove it by pulling it along the roof in a chute made up of boards. The fins of the bomb fouled on an obstruction and the cord broke. He went back to attach a stronger cord and when he pulled it, the bomb exploded.

The next day he had one on the roof of the Ministry of Food. The bomb was without its drogue, so there was no means of attaching a cord, so he made a sling of adhesive tape and, at great risk to himself, placed it around the bomb. The bomb was then lifted out of the roof by means of a cord attached to the sling. It exploded, but was far enough away from the roof for little damage to be sustained.

* * * * * * * * * * *

The other officers of No 3 B D Company who were there at the time were; - The Officer Commanding, Major W G Parker, Lieuts Geoff Birchby, Ross Britain, Cliff Green, Denis Hazell, Eric Wakeling and 2/Lieut Thomas.

On 22nd June, the majority of officers and Sgts were withdrawn from Grimsby, leaving Lieut Eric Wakeling behind to deal with any remaining H.E. bombs as well as any reports of S.D.2's which might come in.

On 23rd he dealt with six. On 24th he dealt with nine in a railway siding. It had been searched and some bombs found, which were disposed of, but no one thought of looking in the railway trucks. It wasn't until a workman started to unload a truck of coal, when an S.D.2 on top of the coal exploded, killing him. Lieut Wakeling was called in to search the trucks and dispose of the bombs. He and his driver climbed up every truck on the sidings and found the nine bombs. Three were on top of loaded wagons and six were lying in the empty trucks. In no way was he going to jump into a truck to examine the fuze of the bomb. Such a bump could set off a (70)B fuze and possibly start a (67) if it had started ticking and stopped, as they often did, just short of the firing time.

He decided to deal with the three on top of the coal. He made a hook out of some strong wire, tied it to a (long) piece of string. Climbed up the end of the first truck and, after three attempts, he managed to get the string to lay over the bomb. Retiring to a safe distance, he pulled the string and the bomb exploded. He was successful with the other two, although they did blow in a few windows of the Railway Station.

Then came the six in the wagons. How to deal with them ? He had, what he thought, was a brilliant idea. With some help, from railway staff, the end truck was unhitched from the rest - Fortunately, it didn't have a bomb in it. - It was pushed up the siding until it reached the points. It was then pushed back, as hard and as fast as possible so that it hit the line of trucks with sufficient force to move each wagon. The result was a satisfactory Bang, Bang, Bang. Three down and three to go.

Lieut Wakeling felt a little more comfortable about jumping into a truck after the treatment the bombs had received. Having waited a precautionary thirty minutes, just in case, he went armed with an explosive charge into each truck, placed it against each of the bombs and fired all three electrically. That gave a better control over each explosion.

On 25th he dealt with three, two on the 26th, 23 on the 27th, two on the 28th, 56 on the 29th, plus an unexploded 50kg phosphorous bomb and seven on the 30th.

The Company War Diary records that on July 2nd 51 were dealt with, a further 51 on July 5th, plus an unexploded 50kg phosphorous bomb and an A.A. Shell. On July 6th eight, on July 7th eight plus two unexploded

50kg phosphorous bombs. Then on July 10th ten followed by five on 11th July. From then to the end of the month 43 more had been dealt plus 13 unexploded 50kg phosphorous bombs.

In August 541 S.D.2's were dealt with and 12 50kg Phosphorous bombs. On 31st he was posted to No 14 B D Company, based in Leeds, although he moved to Hull, following the death of 2/Lt Thomas (See below) and took over the clearance of the S.D.2's North East of Hull.

Well over 100 more S.D.2's were found in the Grimsby area after he left.

* * * * * * * * * * * *

One day whilst working in Lincoln, Lieut Paul Crothall, was returning to his billet, in Wellingore, had 'ticking Fuzes on his mind'. Before he got back, he was stopped by the Police, who advised him that there were 'a few' Butterfly bombs' in a field close by. As there was a path through the field which was used by schoolchildren, he wondered if the bombs could be cleared. So with his Batman/Driver, he set to work, to find the bombs and deal with them. He says;- *"Whilst we were close to one of them, I heard a 'ticking'. Without thinking, I yelled "RUN and later DOWN". I then realised that the (67)B fuze in an S.D.2 does not tick ! Whilst we were lying there, I heard my driver quietly chuckling. I asked what was so funny and he told me that he had recently become the proud possessor of a Russian watch, which had rather a loud tick! I told him to take it off, stick it in his pocket and "Let's get on with it". Which is what we did.*

* * * * * * * * * * * *

There are two recorded fatalities of officers dealing with S.D.2's. The first was the death of Capt Geoffrey Bingham who was 2IC (Second in Command) of the Company at the time.

The site was Epsom Downs, It was a lovely sunny Saturday afternoon and Bingham was disposing of them by blowing them up with a primer. As there was little cover, he 'borrowed' an AFV (Armoured Fighting Vehicle) and installed himself in it when he was actually blowing up the bombs. He thought it advisable to observe each explosion in view of the small charge. (We normally used 1lb Guncotton or a 4 ounce stick of 808) Having set up the explosive charge, he watched through the tiny slit of the AFV when depressing the plunger.

The AFV was at what should have been a safe distance away and Bingham had dealt with a considerable number of these bombs without mishap. Then the 'Million to one' mischance occurred. A fragment of the bomb came through the vision slit and pierced his eye, entering the brain and he was killed instantly.

* * * * * * * * * * * *

An instruction from IF & DBD, dated 17th June 1943, signed by Lt Col G.D. De'ath, reads;- "The enclosed paper on the above subject (Searching for S.D.2's), prepared by the O.C. 22 B.D. Coy, is forwarded for information. The views expressed are those of the author of the paper and will provide a useful basis for discussion on this difficult subject. The paper should be read by all B.D. Officers in preparation for a study period on the subject, a further communication regarding which will be sent later.

22 B.D. Coy was based at Colchester. This was written from the experience gained from a raid which had taken place before the Grimsby one. Essex did suffer S.D. 2 raids earlier in the year, For which a number of awards of the George Medal for bravery were made.

On 1st July IF & DBD put out "Reconnaissance and Disposal of S.D.2 Bombs in Built-up areas." In it were quoted a dozen examples of where bombs were found in Grimsby.

* * * * * * * * * * * *

On 17/18th August 1943, East Yorkshire suffered an S.D.2 raid. Generally referred to as 'the raid on Hull'. In fact, ten villages to the North East of Hull were the recipients. The report was written by Major Alex Cleghorn, who was O.C. 14 B.D. Coy, based at Leeds. - He was rather critical of the Civil Defence efforts to search and record all incidents. He wrote;- "*A check against Police records showed that many more containers and UXB's had been found and marked by the Police than had been reported through Regional H.Q. - The check also showed that whereas only 2 craters had been reported, 65 had in fact been found ! - Regional H.Q. are taking up the matter !*

In 14 Coy's area were a couple of Crusader tanks. Major Cleghorn's report also mentions them;- "It is interesting to note that in a field of corn, being cut by a binder, drawn by a tank, an S.D.2 exploded about one yard ahead of the tank, no doubt due to ground vibration. - In another incident a tank drove over an S.D.2 without exploding it. The tank was backed over it, without a result. Three 4oz sticks of 808 were placed on it, only to drive it further into the ground. FOUR sticks of 808 were finally used, which were successful." The fuze was a (70) B ! - An 'Anti handling fuze'.

It was in this area that the other 'fatality' occurred. It concerned a young 2/Lt who had been posted from 3 B.D. Company, after the Grimsby raid, to 14 B.D. Company, just across the river Humber, at Hull. On 22nd August 2/Lt Thomas went out with L/Sgt Langridge, a L/Cpl and driver clearing Butterfly bombs, which had been dropped on 17/18th. They had gone to a field of stuked corn where one had been reported. The driver of the tractor cutting the corn had been lucky, the tractor wheels had missed it and the reaper blades had passed over the bomb without touching it. This was mainly due to the fact that, because of the wet weather they had been experiencing before the raid, the ground was soft and the bomb, which had lost its drogues, was half buried in the ground.

The fuze was a (67), so it was decided to put a slab of guncotton on it to explode it. This was done, with a length of safety fuze to allow half a minute in which to take cover. Whilst Tommy lit the fuze, the other three went behind a stuke of corn, some 92 yards away and lay down. He then joined them. The guncotton exploded, but the bomb didn't - no one knows why - in fact, because the bomb was half in the ground, it acted as a chute and it went flying up in the air, just 92 yards and landed on the steel helmet of the driver, bounced onto the shoulders of the L/Cpl, then onto the Sgts' bottom and finally, onto Tommy's feet. Then, and only then, did it explode.

Tommy lost his feet and, unfortunately, died of explosive gangrene a few days later. He had been in Bomb disposal for just six months ! The Sgt was wounded, the L/Cpl and driver suffered from shock.

By 10th September 35 containers (All AB 23's) had been found, meaning that 805 bombs should have to be accounted for. Up to then 521 had been destroyed plus 65 craters found, leaving a further 219 to be accounted for.

* * * * * * * * * * * *

Lieut Eric Wakeling said;- "*I didn't arrive until 30th August and as far as I can remember, I was dealing with them for quite some time after. - I wasn't counting them, just blowing them up as they were reported to me..*

One of the fields in which he worked, with his driver, was a field of broad beans. It had been searched by the Home Guard and six bombs were reported. They had been marked with two foot long sticks, but by the time he got there, the beans were three feet high. He and his driver spent an afternoon looking for the six bombs. Having found all of them and the fuzes identified, the (67)'s were dealt with first with explosive - There was always a chance that a (70) would go off in sympathy, thus saving a job ! When the last (70) exploded, they got up, only to fall flat again, as one (unreported and undiscovered) bomb nearby exploded in sympathy. A very wise farmer left that field unpicked, although food was important. It was subsequently re-searched, when the crop had died down. That search revealed another four bombs. Lieut Wakeling and his driver had been walking around that field all afternoon !

* * * * * * * * * * * *

In June 1943, Lieut Paul Crothall was posted from 3 B D Company in Nottingham to No 2 B D Company in London. He relates one of his first jobs on arrival in the Metropolis;-

"I had a job in the sewage farm at Isleworth. (No details of the bomb are given.) When it was finished, I had a very welcome shower - Which was very badly needed ! - The Chief Engineer said he was sorry that he could not offer me anything better, but he could at least give me some of the purest water in the Country !"

* * * * * * * * * * * *

There was a raid on Plymouth on the night of 11/12th August 1943, when a 500kg bomb fell on the corner of Efford Road, thus closing the main road between Exeter and Plymouth.

Most unusually, it was found that the bomb had entered the ground 'TAIL FIRST', through a concrete footpath of a building which had been hit and partially demolished. The bomb had come to rest, partially, uncovered, revealing a ticking (17) fuze. Overhanging the bomb lay a great deal of the partly demolished building and, right over the bomb, suspended by a couple of strands of metal reinforcement, there dangled a piece of concrete, weighing approximately one hundredweight.

Since the remaining roads into Plymouth, from the East were closed, either with bomb craters or unexploded bombs, this bomb was deemed as being 'On the surface' and Lieut John Gray was instructed to 'attempt removal'. Another bomb from the same 'stick' had exploded at 06.00 hours.

Realising that the 'overhang' was in a dangerous condition he decided it would be unwise to attempt to shore it up, because in doing so, some fragments would fall and possibly explode the bomb.

Gas was escaping from a fractured main some three feet from the bomb.

Gray spent four hours, with reliefs from his Sgt, as soon as they felt the effects of the gas upon them. Between them, they scraped away the debris until the fuzes were uncovered. It was difficult as the bomb was not in a 'secure' position and could move at any time. Eventually, they were able to uncover both fuzes and the (50) fuze was immunised. The bomb was then cleared of all debris, put on a truck - with the (17) fuze still ticking, to the bomb cemetery, where it exploded shortly afterwards.

Lieut Gray was awarded the George Medal for his bravery as was Sgt William Bailey who assisted Lieut Gray throughout.

In a period following that raid on Plymouth, Lieut Gray dealt with a further nine bombs, all fitted with (17) and (50) fuzes

* * * * * * * * * * * *

Also on the night of 11/12th August, 57 S.D.2's were dropped on Caston Norfolk. Sgt Brabin of No 3 B D Company disposed of 27 of these, all but one with (70)B fuzes. He found them in fields of corn and in the hedges surrounding them. Many were in very awkward positions. Seven in the hedges, three in corn stukes and 17 in undergrowth.

Later in September and October over 600 more were dropped in the Norfolk area, the majority falling in standing crops of corn, cabbage, sugar beet as well as thick gorse and shrubs on heathland. The majority were fitted with (70)B fuzes, which made the operation particularly hazardous.

For these operations and many others on minefield clearance, Sgt Brabin was awarded the George Medal.

* * * * * * * * * * * *

Following a raid on Norwich in late September, Lieut Kenneth Robinson spent three days from 24th to 26th in the area of Ravenham. He was able to discover and dispose of 79 S.D.2's in heavily wooded countryside with thick undergrowth. Apart from the difficulty in finding them, there was the added problem of actually being able to reach them in order to identify the fuze before deciding whether to tie on a cord or place a charge.

Soon after, an officer of his Company was killed and others sustained injuries when an H.E. bomb which he was trying to immunise exploded. It was assumed to have been one of the new 'Y' fuzes. Lieut Robinson was put in charge of all B D operations in the area. He subsequently reached and immunised seven 500kg bombs, all of which had been fitted with that very sensitive fuze. For these incidents and his work on minefield clearance, he was awarded the George Medal.

* * * * * * * * * * * *

In the December, four 500kg unexploded bombs were reported in the Harlow area. Lieut Swinson, was placed in charge of the clearance of all four. As each one was reached and uncovered, they were all found to be armed with the newly discovered 'Y' fuze. It was decided that two could be detonated in situ, without doing much damage, but the other two had to be rendered safe. He personally dealt with the first and supervised the operations on the second. For this incident, plus those mentioned earlier and a spell on minefield clearance, he was awarded the George Medal.

* * * * * * * * * * * *

Nothing further was reported on the dropping of S.D.2's until May 1944.

* * * * * * * * * * * *

A major engineering job, with sheet steel piling at Wickham Hill Road, Bishops Stortford, to recover a 1000kg bomb

Photo courtesy of Lt Col P S Wadsworth

Inside the shaft at Wickham Hall Road, showing the newly recovered 1000k bomb.

Photo courtesy of Lt Col P S Wadsworth

Chapter Fourteen

1944

At Cuckmere Haven, on 12th February, Lieut J (John) Warren started work on à coastal minefield. The minefield had been laid above a small cliff, which during the war had eroded due to tidal action. Many of the mines were now on the shore and in the fallen cliff, where the mines were out of detector depth. 550 mines were uncovered and made safe, by John Warren, personally, within 12 hours.

* * * * * * * * * * * *

On 19th February there was a heavy raid on London and bombs dropped within one hundred yards of the accommodation billets of No 5 B D Company, who were based at Hampstead. In addition, at 0115 hrs, they received a report that two 250kg and two 500kg bombs had been dropped in the Kentish Town railway sidings. All four were given a Category 'A' priority. Lieut R D Howe, with 108 and 161 B D Sections took on the responsibility of the recovery of all four bombs. By 0900 hrs on 20th they had all been recovered and immunised.

The number of bombs reported as a result of the raid on the 19th was 62. Of that number 21 were Ack Ack shells and 13 were false reports. By the end of the month, the Company had had 136 bombs reported and had dealt with 88 of them, they had also had 34 false reports. - All of which takes the Section Officers considerable time to reconnoitre and took them away from actually dealing with 'real' bombs.

At 13.00 hrs on 23rd February, Lieut J M Gregory received a report of a bomb at Northolt Park Station. By 16.00hrs the following day he, with 108 B D Section had recovered and immunised the bomb.

These were the last few 'jobs' they were to do in the U.K. as soon after they were were part of Operation 'OVERLORD' - the invasion of France.

* * * * * * * * * * * *

On 7th April 1944, Lieut John Warren was detailed to commence work on eight coastal minefields in the Greatstone on Sea area. The type of mine laid was known, but there were no accurate records of the numbers laid or their position or pattern. When originally laid, they had been placed just under the surface in both shingle and the adjoining sandy grassland. Due to to sand drifts and tidal action, the mines were now at depths varying from three feet six inches to 13 feet. The difficulty of searching for the mines was compounded by the fact that existing mine detectors only worked to a depth of just over two feet. In spite of this, at great risk to life, he and his men successfully cleared all the minefields. For his devotion to duty during the above two and other incidents he was awarded the George Medal.

* * * * * * * * * * * *

On 25th April, No 19 B D Company, which had been stationed in New Barnet and had spent much of the past few months in training coupled with some 'construction' jobs. They, too, were part of Operation 'OVERLORD'.

* * * * * * * * * * * *

A report by the O.C. No 6 B.D. Coy who had just taken over the command, Major W G (Paddy) Parker. MBE., reads; "*There were two raids, on consecutive nights. On 6/7th May 1944 it was on Bovington Camp and*

Kimmeridge. The following night East Lulworth and Winfrith Heath were hit. Both raids were a mixture of S.D.2's, S.D.10's and some 50kg phosphorous bombs.

It is interesting to note that a new type of container was used. It being an AB70-3 which held 22 S.D.2's. Eight containers were used - 172 bombs - on Bovington Camp plus 148 S.D.10A's. These were carried in AB500-1's, each holding 37 bombs.

The Police carried out the search for the UXB's without much assistance from the Military occupants of the camp ! The camp did not possess any sandbags either. The Police supplied 1000 during the first day and the military managed to rustle up 500. Paddy Parker 'demanded', and got, 50 men from the camp who were put to work under the instruction of personnel from 99 B.D. Section.

Four S.D.2's were found in the REME workshop and were dealt with without damage to the vehicles. However, two bombs were actually embedded in the wall of the building. The resultant explosion created a five foot diameter hole. A number were found in the Married Quarters area. 18 were dealt with, without damage to property. On the following day a number were dealt with in the NAAFI, again without damage. In all 154 bombs were accounted for.

At Kimmeridge, 132 S.D.2's were dropped along with 111 S.D.10's and six 50kg Phosphorous. Incredibly all the bombs were found in open country in an area some 800 yards long and 120 yards wide. Within two days it had been searched and marked by the Police. As the ground was flat, affording no protection, a trench was dug and covered over, to provide head protection. 52 out of the 64 bombs with 70B fuzes were exploded by pulling on a string. Six bombs were fitted with 41 fuzes. These and the 'failed' 70B's were detonated using 4 ozs of 808 explosive, with a 1 oz Guncotton primer and safety fuze. The whole operation took seven and a half hours.

In all 70 bombs were disposed of, five were detonated by cattle, which were put into the field before the farmer realised there had been a raid. A further 3 cows were killed along with a bull and a cow so badly injured that they had to be destroyed.

* * * * * * * * * * * *

On May 3rd, some eleven months after they had been dropped, two S.D.2's were discovered in a Grimsby cemetery.

* * * * * * * * * * * *

Lieut D L (Don) Anderson was still with No 4 B.D Company which was now based in North London, covering part of London. He met some Americans who were on General Eisenhowers 'Rainbow H Q staff'. "*I took then to a Home Guard Ack Ack Battery in Hyde Park where they were trying to shoot the cornice off the Grosvenor Hotel. On our way back I found the contents of a Bloomsbury Hotel standing in the rain in the street, because 'There was an unexploded bomb in their dining room.' I discovered that it was an Ack Ack shell lodged in the ceiling, obligingly displaying the fact that it was set at 'Safe' ! I pulled it out of the ceiling and told them all to go back to bed.*

On my way to the front door, I was stopped by an ARP warden. I explained what had happened and that I was returning the shell to the battery from which it had been fired. "This is MY Sector" he announced firmly "and this is MY incident; if you want an incident, go out and find one of your own". He insisted that I put it back where I found it and then he fetched all the hotel guests and staff back into the rain !

* * * * * * * * * * * *

At 0015 hrs on 8th May a single plane dropped a mixed load of 110 S.D.2's in AB 70 containers, 74 S.D.10A's and two 50kg Phosphorous. The area affected was a group of 12 houses, a public house, a school and the road through the area, which was closed to traffic. Five houses were evacuated on account of damage caused by one S.D.10 and an AB 500 container and some of its contents of S.D.10's which also exploded.

The Police had the area searched by early afternoon, reporting 102 S.D.2's and 54 S.D.10's. The fuzing of the S.D.2's was equally split between 41's and 70B's. There were seven bombs on the road and these were dealt with as a priority. On the following day, Lt Evans had disposed of 95 S.D.2's. He also defused eight unarmed fuzes from a container which had only opened very near the ground.

Winfrith Heath was RAF property and the search and clearance was carried out by the local Bomb Disposal Flight of the RAF.

On 19th June 1944, The GOC South Eastern Command sent out an instruction to:- East Kent District, Sussex District, Aldershot District, and North Kent & Surrey District, Referring to their *OVERLORD* Operational Instructions. It was obvious that the 'Powers that be' were very concerned about the possibility of the build up of troop concentrations in the area could be a prime target. A copy of Lt Col Parker's report to IF & DBD was attached, as was another appendix detailing the bomb itself and the methods of searching and marking.

Had the Germans decided to 'swamp' the Assembly areas with S.D.2's at that time, Operation 'OVERLORD' would probably have never happened. The chaos caused by thousands of 'Butterfly Bombs' in an area full of men and vehicles is unimaginable. Grimsby was brought to a standstill for several days by just 2,700 bombs. I still maintain that the secrecy of the effects of the raid on Grimsby paid dividends. If the enemy had realised just what chaos they caused, they would have been producing the Butterfly Bomb by the 'Millions'. The Allies knew that. Not only the British Army and, of course the USA, but Russia was also let into the secret and produced their own.

* * * * * * * * * * * *

Two days later, Capt A B (Alwyn - usually known as 'A B') Waters, of No 23 B D Company, was asked to assist Flt Lt Gillett in clearing a 'C' type parachute mine. On arrival at the reported site, they found the mine just ten yards from the main road. Capt Waters was a skilled B D Officer and was fully aware that the mine was fitted a new type of fuze and that his equipment might not be up to immunising it. He was also aware that he could have called in the Royal Navy experts, but such action would have meant a delay of at least two hours before the nearest Mine Safety Officer could arrive. Such a delay could cause untold damage and casualties. He asked Flt Lt Gillett to lay out a cord, for the removal of the fuze by remote control and then ordered him to retire to a safe distance. Capt Waters then applied the standard drill to remove the fuze, which he knew by the markings was booby trapped. He retired 100 yards and was able to remove the fuze, without the mine exploding. After waiting for a reasonably safe time, he returned to the mine, to recover the fuze. When he picked it up, he found it to be ticking and before he could take any action, it exploded, severely injuring his foot. A George Medal was added to his already awarded MBE.

* * * * * * * * * * * *

Numbers 23, 24 and 25 B D Companies, all of whom had been withdrawn from U.K. B D Operations for some time, for training and reorganisation, went to France as part of Operation 'OVERLORD'.

* * * * * * * * * * * *

Lieut P (Phillip) Hennings, of No 12 B D Company, was engaged in minefield clearance in early 1944 when he was given the job of clearing certain minefields on the South Coast, prior to 'D' Day. It was, of course, imperative that these minefields should be cleared with EVERY mine being accounted for. No risks could be taken when the invasion forces used these beaches. In spite of the fact that no accurate plans existed and also that they had been subjected to tidal waters, he and his men successfully removed over 2,500 beach mines, without loss of life. For this and other incidents, he was awarded the George Medal.

* * * * * * * * * * * *

Major W G Parker, MBE, already mentioned as Commanding No 16 B D Company. In spite of this he was involved in the clearance of a minefield, showing great initiative and ingenuity very much needed at the time due to rather heavy losses experienced by the Company. One minefield, near an ammunition magazine at Corsham, Wilts. There were only 16 mines, but they were laid in a dark tunnel some 150 fifty feet long. It was so dangerous that he decided to deal with it himself. The mines were Anti Tank Mines Mk I, fitted with No 5 Trap Mechanism. The main problem was that it was not known at what pressure the mines would explode, owing to the time that had expired since they had been laid in 1940. Major Parker, in the dim artificial light provided, uncovered and made safe all the mines. A George Medal was added to his MBE.

* * * * * * * * * * * *

Lieut R A J (Robert) Woods was also in No 16 B.D Company and worked with Major Parker on the S.D.2's at Bovington Camp. Apart from that incident, his diary for the years was interesting and, in a way, typical of the variety of jobs which were falling to the lot of the B D Officer at that time.

One of the anti invasion measures put into place was designed to deny the use of airfields to the enemy - apart from sticking poles in large fields which could be used as glider landing grounds. Airfields needed to be used, by the RAF, but in the event of an invasion, we should have the ability to deny their use to the enemy. 'Pipe Mines' were the answer. Sometimes called

'McNaughton tubes', they were pipes about the size of scaffold tubing, filled with explosive, usually gelignite.

In January, Lieut Woods removed 48 pipe mines from Hurn Airport. They varied in length from 20 to 60 feet. In the February, he removed 32 from Lee on Solent airfield. Between March and June he dealt with 73 H.E. bombs in Weymouth, Portland and the Dorset area and over 200 S.D.2's.

On 3rd June he went into a minefield at Tilly Whim Caves, near Swanage, to recover the bodies of two Canadian Air Force Officers. He personally, worked his way in with a Mine Detector, marking all the mines as he went. He successfully removed the bodies although one was almost on top of a mine.

August/September found him working on the coastal minefields, clearing 117 Beach Type 'C' mines in one minefield and 317 anti personnel mines in a minefield at Abbottsbury. For his continuous bravery over many months, he was awarded the George Medal.

* * * * * * * * * * * *

On 24th June, Major J P (John) Hudson MBE. GM. assisted by Mr Hurst, Dr Dawson and others, went to Strawberry Hill farm, Staplecross, Sussex, where a Flying Bomb had come to rest, without exploding. They had come to investigate the fuzing system of the first complete flying bomb to become 'available'.

Two of the three fuzes were similar to those found on previously recovered, but incomplete bombs and were dealt with by Major Hudson. However, there was a third fuze contained in a rear side fuze pocket. It was unmarked and unknown ! Major Hudson was instructed by D.B.D. (Director of Bomb Disposal) to recover it at all costs.

Fortunately, Radiography was now available, which meant that the inside of a fuze could be shown up on a plate, similar to that of an X Ray. It showed the existence of a clockwork mechanism, similar to that in a normal (17) fuze.

An attempt to obtain a clearer radiograph, by placing an improvised film holder in the front side fuze pocket gave negative results and it was decided to remove portions of the bomb casing, either side of the fuze pocket, then to dissolve some of the explosive, with a view to placing the film and source in contact with the fuze pocket, to obtain maximum clarity.

The fuze was presumed to be in an 'armed' condition and to have a short time setting. (Both assumptions proved to be correct) The danger under such circumstances was that the clock could start (or restart) due to an extremely small disturbance. The bomb casing was cut by using acid, have earlier experimented on another Flying Bomb casing !

The operation took five hours, being shared between Major Hudson and Mr Hurst. They had already been warned about the inadvisability of allowing the acid to reach the explosive ! And so the acid treatment had to be stopped before it cut completely through the casing. A case of 'nice judgement !' The case was finally cut with a sharp knife.

The explosive around the fuze pocket was dissolved away by all three men, working in short shifts as the toxic effect caused dizziness, vomiting and extreme lassitude on the part of the operators, coupled with an ashen pallor and blue lips. Between them, they worked for 13 hours.

Dr Dawson set up the 'Field Photography', with a source on one side of the fuze pocket and a plate on the other. The resulting film showed that the movement was similar to that of an earlier fuze, giving a maximum two hour delay and that no anti withdrawal device was fitted. But it did not disclose how much of the two hours the clock had run.

The next step was the withdrawal of the fuze. As this could not be done without vibration which could cause a restart of the clock, Major Hudson and Mr Hurst devised a 'remote control extractor'. Whilst Mr Hurst listened on the stethoscope, some 50 yards away, Major Hudson worked the controls from a distance of 100 yards. The fuze was successfully extracted and, by an ingenious arrangement, was allowed to swing into a strong magnetic field which would effectively prevent the fuze from restarting. (Or stop it, if it had restarted.) Major Hudson removed the gaine from the fuze, which on testing was found to be fully armed but not started and set to operate at 32 minutes.

This operation started on 24th June and went on almost continuously, during the hours of daylight, until 17.00 hrs 2nd July. During this time flying bombs continued to fly overhead, as well as dropping close by, which was cause of concern, in case the shock of a bomb exploding nearby would start the clock.

There is no doubt that Major Hudson's work on this and many other incidents had placed him in great danger. Nevertheless his technical excellence and technical observations under extreme circumstances were of the highest order and contributed in no small degree to the German Fuzing system and how to deal with them.

For this he was awarded his second George Medal.

* * * * * * * * * * * *

Prior to 'D' Day, Capt P F (Paul) Crothall went on a Diving Course at Chatham - under R.N. tuition ! *We were using American diving suits. I went down 4 or 5 fathoms and immediately felt very cold water coming up my arms. We had to do everything by hand signals so, with my legs fast filling up with water, I signalled 'Pull me up'. As soon as I got to the side of the boat a gruff Naval Instructor removed my facepiece and said "What the bloody hell is wrong with you ?" I explained and he immediately said to his assistant "Give him a couple more pairs of Greys." As soon as they were fitted my facepiece was replaced and I was sent down again, with the ice cold water still around*

166

my legs ! No sympathy, whatsoever from the Royal Navy! He was later to be awarded an MBE for his bravery in France.

* * * * * * * * * * * *

In the July, Lieut E W (Eric) Sivil was called away from his work of minefield clearance. Whilst the threat of an invasion had disappeared - we were now invading France ! - It was at the height of the V1 bombing. Very few of these missiles failed to explode. However, Lieut Sivil was despatched to immunise one which had fallen in No B D 20 Company area. (Kent & Sussex). It was the first time he had ever seen one 'close up' ! All he knew about them was what he had read in various B D Instructions, which we received regularly, to update us on the latest German trickery. So armed with the 'instructions' he applied his 'expertise' and was successful in immunising it, without blowing himself up. For this incident and his bravery on the minefields, he was awarded the George Medal.

* * * * * * * * * * * *

In the July, No 14 B D Company took delivery of over 1,000 German Tellermines, which had been shipped back from North Africa. It was their job to remove the explosive from the mines so that they could be used for training purposes. It fell to Lieut Eric Wakeling to organise and carry out the operation.

A site was chosen on the outskirts of Leeds - a sloping field. With the quantity of mines to be emptied, it was decided to use two Steam Sterilizers. Two level plots were dug for the machines and their water supply tanks. Water was obtained from a nearby hydrant in the road bordering the field. A metered standpipe was supplied by the local Water Company who required payment for all the water that was used.

Two pits were dug for the actual operations. Two 'trepanners' were used to cut a two inch hole in the base of the mines. An adaptation had to be made in the unit

167

workshop to allow the trepanners to be used. The base of the mine was flat and about 16 inches in diameter, whereas the bombs for which they were designed were cylindrical and could be up to 30 inches in diameter.

Channels were then dug from the working pits, to allow the molten explosive to drain away, into further pits, where it was allowed to solidify. At the end of the operation, which took several days, it was dug up and put into sandbags and finally burnt.

The entire operation was a messy business. The whole area was a mass of steam, which carried a certain amount of explosive in it. All those working on the site inhaled the explosive laden steam, which lead to bronchial and lung problems. The handling of the explosive also caused Impetigo. They were all extremely pleased when the operation was completed.

＊＊＊＊＊＊＊＊＊＊＊＊

On 2nd August, the HQ of No 14 B D company in Leeds, received a report that there had been an accident in a minefield at Redcar and that there had been some deaths. Lieut H W (Harry) Beckingham was immediately despatched to the site, arriving late in the evening. The Officer in charge, Lieut Stewart, plus his Sgt and two sappers had been killed and their bodies, or what remained of them were still in the minefield. Apart from ensuring that the minefield was sealed and the men who were suffering from shock, received the necessary treatment, there was little he could do that night.

On the following morning he returned to the minefield and made an inspection of the carnage. Returning to the barracks, he laid down the instructions to the men who would be going back into the minefield to recover the bodies. He wanted no more accidents. Instruction finished, he took the men back, opened up the field and went in with a mine detector, sweeping a path to the nearest body. Two sappers followed him, with tapes to mark out the 'clean' area. It took some hours to complete the work, but the remains of all the bodies were collected and taken to the Mortuary.

Most of the minefield had erupted and it took a long time to plot every crater against the minefield chart and to work out just how many mines there were left to clear - and where they were. Lieut Eric Wakeling returned to the minefield, later, with a more efficient detector (The E R A Locator) than the PMD (Polish Mine Detector) and was able to account for every unexploded mine and declare the area safe.

* * * * * * * * * * * *

Lieut L H (Taffy) Morgan had been working on the minefields since he joined No 7 B D Company in the September. On 8th December he was in charge of a party working on a very difficult minefield at Wyke Regis, when there was an explosion and an NCO was killed. Lieut Morgan although badly injured, attended to the needs of other personnel whose injuries were even more serious. He entered the live part of the minefield to remove the injured and the body of the dead NCO, whose body was badly mutilated. He later continued on the clearance of the minefield. The award of the George Medal was not announced in the London Gazette until after the war - 5th October 1945.

* * * * * * * * * * * *

Late in 1944, No 6 B D Company, whose O.C. was now Major W G Parker MBE GM, was reformed, and reorganised, to go to the Far East. The unit was broken down into 'Light' Platoons. Each commanded by a Captain with a Lieut as Second in Commnad and about 29 other ranks. Their H.Q. was Great Ballard House, New Milton. Hants.

Some of the sections were sent to France in April 1945, whilst the remainder of the Company sailed for a war with Japan. Fortunately, for them, the war had ended by the time they got to India.

Some of the exploits of those who went to France are in a following chapter.

A Japanese 50 kg Incendiary bomb, recovered from Burma by Lt G R Ovens in 1942.
Photo Courtesy of Capt G R Ovens TD.

Officers of No 6 B D Company RE, April 1945, outside Great Ballard House, New Milton.
Back row (L - R) Lt Warren, Lt Wilson, Lt C Walker, ?.
Front Row Capt Pollock, Capt J Hirst, Capt W Bishop, Major W G Parker MBE GM, Capt Ledoyen, Capt E Sivil, Lt Best.
Photo courtesy of Capt C Walker.

Two views of the beach minefield clearance operation at Brighton, using a 'bulldozer' to uncover the 'B' type C mines laid in 1940.
Both photos courtesy of Col B S T Archer GC OBE ERD

172

Chapter FIFTEEN

MALTA

Malta had it's first air raid on 11th June 1940.

Capt J H Jephson-Jones and Lieut W M Eastman, both of the Royal Army Ordnance Corps, were in Malta, but there were no Bomb Disposal Units. Both were trained Armament Officers, but without any knowledge of German or Italian bombs. Between them they dismantled all the UXB's, to find out how they worked and then set up an 'Ad Hoc' unit of volunteers from both the RAOC and RE. They were helped by an RE Corporal named C A Brewer and two sappers whose names were W D Scott and D MacDonald. All of whom were 'borrowed' from No 24 Fortress Company RE. Their disposal problems differed from those in the U.K. in that most bombs failed to penetrate the rocky ground in Malta and so they were found on the surface. They were both awarded the George Cross for their continued efforts in the early day and both ended their Army Careers as Brigadiers.

It was not until November when the first experienced RE Bomb Disposal officer was sent out from the U.K. Lieut E E (Eric) Talbot, was that officer, who had already been awarded the George Cross for his earlier bravery in 1940. He brought with him all the latest knowledge and equipment available, regarding German fuzes and their immunisation. This was very fortunate as the Luftwaffe began its raids again, having been withdrawn earlier for the Russian front offensive.

With the arrival of Lieut Talbot, the B D organisation was put on a more regular footing and by December 1942 their numbers increased to 30. Almost all of them were commended for their bravery at one time or another. It was then that the Sappers took over, 'borrowing' men from No 24 Fortress Squadron RE.

Sadly, Lieut Talbot was killed in October 1941, when he was enjoying some time off and a little relaxation by having a flight in an RAF aircraft which, unfortunately, was shot down and all were killed.

Lt Talbot was replaced by Lieut T W T (Thomas) Blackwell, who already had been awarded the MBE, to take charge of B D Operations on the island. He immediately set about reorganising the set up and established two B D Sections, Nos 127 and 128. They became separate units from No 24 Fortress Company. Although most of the men still considered themselves to be part of the Company. Lieut Blackwell was awarded the George Medal for his untiring efforts and heroism throughout the worst of the Malta bombing.

* * * * * * * * * * * *

During a raid on the night of 30th July, at around 22.00 hrs several delayed action bombs were dropped, one of which was in a very built up area, burying a number of civilians.

When he arrived at the scene Lieut Blackwell found the bomb partially exposed with two (17) fuzes (Delayed action) both of which were ticking. He decided that the best action would be to remove the bomb so that work could continue to rescue the entombed people. However, there was a problem, one just doesn't pick up a 550lb bomb and walk away with it, and no lifting gear was available, so it was decided to tow it away.

It was first necessary to clear a passage for the bomb. In this he was ably assisted by P.C. Baylis, a local constable. The bomb was hitched to a vehicle, but the street only permitted a tow rope length of 12 feet. The first attempt failed because the bomb got stuck in some debris. It was then decided that two people were required, one to drive the truck and the other to guide the bomb ! P.C. Baylis volunteered to drive the truck, which left Lieut Blackwell to guide the bomb. They were successful in reaching the area chosen for its (temporary) 'home'.

Whilst they were carrying out this operation another bomb from this raid exploded. For this operation and for many others performed during his tour on the island, he was awarded the George Medal.

It is sad to report that of those buried in the building from which he had removed the bomb, no one was recovered alive.

Unfortunately, the report on Lieut Blackwell does not tell us whether P.C. Baylis was awarded a well deserved George Medal.

* * * * * * * * * * * *

Another George Medal was awarded to L/Sgt R C M (Reg) Parker, who assisted Lieut Blackwell with a 2,000lb bomb which had come to rest, wedged in a doorway of a very congested area. A new type of cap was found to cover the fuze and a booby trap was suspected. The fuze was underneath and it was necessary to turn the bomb over, by hand. an operation in which Sgt Parker was particularly prominent.

On two other occasions he worked on clearing aerodromes of UXB's after heavy attacks. Owing to the urgent necessity of getting the runways fir for use, many of the safety precautions were were ignored.

* * * * * * * * * * * *

In 1949 Lieut C V (Charles) Sadler was posted to Malta, where he stayed until 1953. Whilst he was there, one of the bombs he dealt with was a 500kg armour piercing bomb, which had fallen in the Royal Navy Dockyard and recovered in 1950. Obviously the bombs which did penetrate the rockhard surface on the island, took quite a time to reach and recover.

* * * * * * * * * * * *

Whilst Lieut Sadler was there, he was called out one night by a Wing Commander Beaumont, who had a ship in the harbour, but was frightened to sail as he had found some explosives in the bilges. On reaching the harbour Lieut Sadler was conducted to a Coaster of about 1,000 tons. He walked up the gangplank in a dim light to be met by two burly ruffians, who took him to the Wing Commander's cabin. He also happened to be the Captain of the ship.

The Wing Commander took him down below and there, around the prop shaft were packed bundles of cordite. They were obviously the propellant of shells. Lieut Sadler told Beaumont that he would be back in the morning to make a proper inspection. On leaving the ship he immediately got in touch with the Duty Security Officer.

Next morning, at first light the dock was sealed off by UK troops and the ship boarded. The Captain and his crew of four were all arrested and the ship impounded. Simultaneously, the Maltese Ammunition depot was raided and a number of people arrested. There it was found that a large number of 'propellant tubes' contained no cordite whatsoever. Some were even being emptied at the time of the raid.

Wing Commander Beaumont had never seen the RAF. He was, in fact, an Ex Borstal boy and was very much involved in arms running to the Middle East.

The next day, Mrs Beaumont presented herself. She was stranded with two children. She was taken to Welfare and found accommodation and a passage back to the UK. She was, in fact, the daughter of a Gloucestershire Vicar and a very nice person, who had been taken in by a plausible rogue.

176

Lt E E Talbot GC with members of his Bomb Disposal Section, 'borrowed' from No 24
Fortress Company RE, in Malta 1942
Photo courtesy of Spr G Fielding

Malta, 1950. Loading a 500kg bomb on the back of a truck. A combined Services job,
with the Royal Navy assisting.

177

Two photos of Capt C V Sadler, with his Section at Malta, with some of the unexploded missiles recovered by his section.
Photos courtesy of Capt C V Sadler.

178

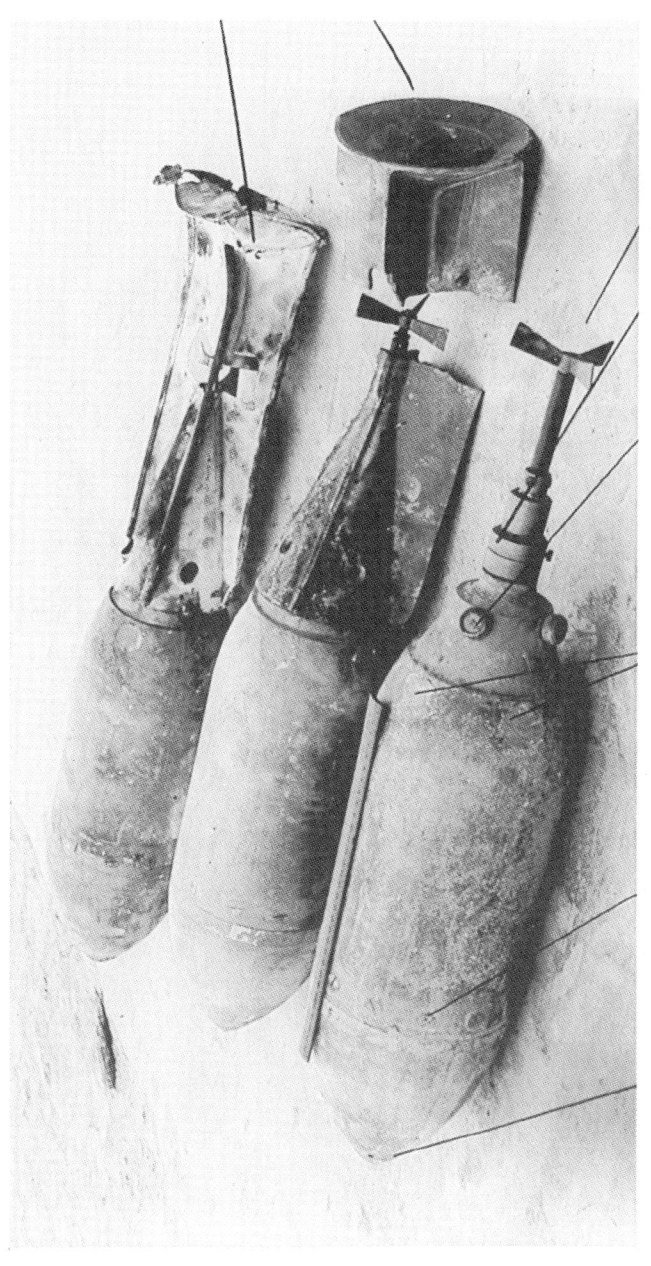

Italian 20kg Incendiary Bombs, dropped on Malta. Photo courtesy of Capt C V Sadler.

Officers of No 24 B D Company, circa 1944
Photo courtesy of Capt P Crothall MBE

Chapter Sixteen

NORTH AFRICA AND ITALY

No 18 B D Company was formed at Halifax on 1st November 1940, with a Major R W Johnstone as O.C. They were soon posted to the Middle East, where they remained for the rest of the war, being joined by another Company in 1941, followed by three more Companies when the invasion of North Africa took place.

In July 1941, No 28 B D Company was formed, at Chelsea, in London. Another record shows it as being formed in the Middle East, from a nucleus of volunteer Officers and Senior NCO's, from a range of Regiments. It also records they had little or no bomb disposal experience, but then, neither did the newly formed Companies in the U.K. in June of 1940.

Major G H Bradbury was it's first O C. and by 20th, the HQ and three sections - Numbered 111, 112 and 113 were mobilized for overseas and issued with 'tropical' gear. Early in August sections numbered 114, 115 and 116 were also mobilized.

On 25th August they all moved to their Port of Embarkation and duly arrived in North Africa to support No 18 B D Company, which, at the time was considerably overstretched.

* * * * * * * * * * * *

In November 1942, Nos 8 and 15 B D Companies came from the U.K. to land with the invasion forces in

North Africa. No 17 B D Company mobilized for North Africa in March 1943.

＊ ＊ ＊ ＊ ＊ ＊ ＊ ＊ ＊ ＊ ＊ ＊

Between 27th May and 12th September 1941, Captain J B (James) Smith, Royal Engineers, displayed gallantry and continued devotion to duty at Mersa Matruh, without thought of personal safety. He undertook the most hazardous work in the investigation, defuzing and subsequent removal and destruction of several hundred enemy UXB's of all types, sizes and weights, up to 1000kg. One such bomb was found at 20 feet and another at 28 feet. On 29th August he dealt with two 250kg bombs, thus preventing the demolition of several buildings and later he made safe two Italian sea mines.

In every case, it was Capt Smith who visited the site of a reported UXB, before any one else was allowed near it.

He was awarded the George Medal for his continual bravery.

＊ ＊ ＊ ＊ ＊ ＊ ＊ ＊ ＊ ＊ ＊ ＊

Early in 1944, there began a concerted effort to dispose of the German Ammunition dumps in North Africa, led by a team from the Royal Air Force. Major P J (John) Hands was then O.C. of No 18 B D Company which, along with No 28 B D Company, were tasked with reconnoitring and the disposal of all the enemy bomb dumps. By now there was No 4 (Indian) Bomb Disposal Company R E. in the area. Which was by far the largest B D unit but less mobile and so they were given the bulk of the demolition jobs. By the September No 18 B D Company had cleared most of the larger and more important dumps along the main coast road and were now in Tripoli. The next job was in the area of Hun. With the assistance of a local 'Caid', John Hands and his team were led to an Italian depot, where they found the bombs, mainly 200kg in neat and tidy stacks in a number of huts. There was only one problem - they were all booby trapped. Having dealt with such a problem in the past, he decided to show Lieut Murray, of the South African Army, how the booby traps should be defuzed.

He proceeded to demonstrate the method and was almost finished when, out of the corner of his eye, he saw another pair of hands copying his movements. They were the hands of a Bedouin. It was too late to shout and the Bedouin blew himself up, along with most of the hut. John Hands was blown through the roof of the store into the minefield outside. Lieut Murray lost a leg. Sgt Campbell pulled Lieut Murray out of the still burning building whilst Driver Reece drove his Jeep into the minefield to rescue John Hands, which he did without exploding a mine.

Both injured men were airlifted to hospital. Hands had 23 pieces of metal removed from his back and stomach.

* * * * * * * * * * * *

Driver W Reece was awarded the George Medal for his heroic efforts. His citation reads;- *On 6th September 1944, at Hun, Tripolitania, Driver W (Wilfred) Reece, RASC, was attached to 18 B D Company RE was one of a number of drivers left in an oasis for vehicle maintenance. An explosion occurred in an enemy ammunition dump which was being examined by the Officer Commanding, Major P J Hands and another officer. Reece immediately drove to the scene of the explosion where he found one officer injured in the, now, burning magazine and was informed that the O.C. was in the minefield.*

He unhestitatingly controlled the approach of the other drivers to the area and went into the minefield and carried out the O.C. who was lying injured inside.

Shortly after, the first 40 and subsequently 200 tons of bombs exploded. Reece's action undoubtedly saved Major Hands' life. For which he was awarded the George Medal.

* * * * * * * * * * * *

There were two George Medals awarded for Bomb Disposal Bravery in the subsequent Italian campaign, both to officers of No 17 B D Company.

Between 2nd and 9th October 1943, Lieut James Allen defused and removed seven British bombs fitted with both long delay fuze and anti handling devices. The bombs were adjacent to the Salerno/Naples railway and were impeding military operations. It was also important that they did not explode in situ.

The British long delay fuze and anti handling devices were much more difficult to immunise than the German versions and had already caused a great number of casualties. Great courage and ingenuity was required. In fact, Air Ministry Instructions laid down that all bombs so fuzed, should be exploded in situ. In spite of this Lieut Allen accepted the risks, thus avoiding serious hindrance to operations.

Between 9th and 15th October, he and his section were in Naples employed on the 'delousing' of buildings. i.e., the clearance of booby traps. In that time 85 were found and defuzed. At Piedmont Barracks, which had previously been declared 'safe' by other troops, an explosion occurred killing 25 American soldiers. Allen checked two barracks, disconnected and neutralised a German firing mechanism connected to 1,590 pounds of high explosive.

* * * * * * * * * * * *

His colleague Lieut Kenneth Lanham had been busy earlier at Taranto. Between 18th September and 16th October he defuzed six British bombs, all fitted with the long delay fuzes and anti handling devices. Again, the bombs could not be exploded in situ, without seriously interfering with both Naval and Military operations. One bomb was by a main aqueduct, four were on the main railway line and one was in a gasworks.

* * * * * * * * * * * *

Lieut Cruden, Sgt Brinton and men of No 61 B D Section with an S.C. 500kg bomb, which they had just recovered.

Photo courtesy of Sgt C E Brinton

A 1000kg bomb, recovered from under an outhouse, in Eaton Road, Richmond. Surrey. (L to R) WOII Moore, POW, POW, QMS Jones, Capt Sharp, Capt Wadsworth, POW, POW.
Photo courtesy of Lt Col P S Wadsworth.

186

Chapter Seventeen

FRANCE

On 11th June 1944 a ship carrying stores and men to the Normandy beaches received a direct hit with a bomb which failed to explode. A number of men were injured and the ships steering gear damaged. The ship was carrying some 650 men, with a full load of vehicles and equipment.

The bomb, which was thought to be a 1200 kg 'Glider' bomb, had come to rest in the coal bunker and was likely to explode at any minute.

Capt A G (Arthur) Burdett of 756 Field Company RE asked the Ship's Captain for permission to make an attempt to render the bomb safe, to which he agreed. Taking with him Cpl F J (Fred) Jackson, who had had some B D experience, they set off for the bomb, which was found amidst the coal and which was constantly shifting with the motion of the ship.

Working under great difficulties, including the darkness of their surroundings and their lack of knowledge of the bomb and its fuzing, they eventually succeeded in making it safe.

The bomb was then moved to a position under a hatch where with the aid of the ship's derrick it was lifted and dropped overboard.

There is no doubt that their courageous action saved the ship and its valuable cargo from total destruction, for which they were both awarded the George Medal.

* * * * * * * * * * * *

After 'D' Day, 24 B D Coy was attached to the Canadian Army. They were good hosts and looked after the unit well. Frequently asking after their welfare, even to the extent of the Divisional Commander personally visiting them to see what they needed.

Some time later they were warned of a 2000 bomber raid on Caen by the Allies - It was a sight to behold ! - One would have thought that no one could have survived such a raid, but there were still snipers around and some German Ack Ack batteries were still working.

At the time the unit was in dugouts in the Botanical Gardens in Caen where they were molested by mosquitos. The M.O. thought he had seen the worst in the Far East, but those in Caen beat them hollow ! They used to put 'Anti gas ointment' on their skin but this did not deter the insects.

One day the Canadians came along to ask if they could borrow a couple of pumps. Having been such good hosts, they could not be refused.

Some days later they came back carrying two Jerricans and, the British, assuming that the Jerricans contained water, duly thanked the Canadians, although there was no shortage of water. They were told; 'This ain't water' - It's got a kick like a mule ! It was only then that they were told of a warehouse full of every possible sort of liquor which had been flattened in the bombing. Any unbroken bottles had been 'recovered' by the Canadians ! BUT, in the cellars there was about a two feet depth of mixed drinks, which the Canadians had pumped out, filtered five times, then put into Jerricans !! The mules certainly kicked very hard !!

There were three 1000 pounders to dispose of from the sides of the runway at Aurich Airfield. Notices were placed in both English and German. The RAF were also warned as to when they would be detonated, but apparently they were over keen to have a looksee and had a considerable 'uplift' when they flew over at the time of the explosion.

The three fuzes had been lit and the demolition team were all making their way back to the foxhole when, to their horror, they saw an old farmer driving a horse and cart in the direction of the bombs. There was certainly no time to go back and remove the fuzes and they expected to find a nasty mess after the explosion. When everything which went up had come down again, through the clearing dust they saw the farmer still continuing in his original direction. *(One lucky and probably deaf old man.)*

The Canadians wanted to celebrate Queen Victoria's birthday with a firework display. The airfield was pock marked with craters and the B D Company filled some of them with various explosive devices found in the German airfield stores, including magnesium flares, oil bombs, etc., All of which put up a very good show. So much so that the Divisional Commander, who was about 16 miles away and had seen the sky light up came over to have a look and stayed !!

* * * * * * * * * * * *

Corporal William Jones was in No 5 B D Company, stationed near the village of Orbois, France. He was part of a platoon of that Company, detailed to clear the mines and booby traps in the village, where there had been at least four accidents to both civilians and soldiers, due to the booby traps. Between the dates of 3rd to 7th September he cleared eleven booby traps, two of which were in a very sensitive condition.

On the following day there was an accident in a minefield of 'Schu' mines. His Section officer was severely injured and both the Platoon Sgt and L/Sgt were casualties. In spite of this, Cpl Jones continued the clearance of the minefield, although the Section Officer had expressed doubts about the viabiliy of the equipment they were using. On 12th Sept a L/Cpl and a sapper were killed in the same minefield. Cpl Jones took charge and work continued. Clearance was further hampered by fallen branches and various pieces of equipment, with which the area was littered. For his leadership and a high devotion to duty, he was awarded the George Medal.

* * * * * * * * * * * *

Whilst Cpl Jones was working on the booby traps in Orbois, Lieut Ronald Walker, of the same B D Company, 'came across' a captured enemy document, which recorded a large minefield of 'Schu' mines in the Orbois area. In view of the casualties already experienced by the Company and the doubt which was being expressed about the Mk IV mine detector, Lieut Walker volunteered to work in the minefield to restore confidence in the NCO's and men. Unfortunately, his bravery was rewarded by an exploding 'Schu' mine, which amputated his left foot and caused permanent injury to his right eye. He was awarded the George Medal for his bravery.

* * * * * * * * * * * *

On 6th November, at Hassault, the reconstruction of a demolished railway bridge was stopped owing to the presence of a UXB - under 30 feet of water in the Albert Canal.

Lieut George Gaylor, of No 23 B D Company, went down in a diving suit and found the bomb, half buried in mud underneath torn railway lines, steel girders and wreckage.

To do this, he had to squeeze himself between damaged girders at the risk of tearing his diving suit, fouling the air line or catching his life line in the debris, thus being trapped.

In spite of nil visibility, he was able to identify the fuze by torch. Since none of the existing immunising systems would work under water, he removed the fuze without immunising it - a dangerous action. - Due to the mud and the damaged condition of the bomb he was not able to ascertain whether there was a second fuze. He was able to attach a rope to the bomb and it was brought to the surface. Fortunately, when the bomb reached the surface and was cleaned, there was not a second fuze.

For his efforts in enabling work to continue of the reconstruction, he was awarded the George Medal.

* * * * * * * * * * * *

Now in France, Sgt Brinton, who had earlier been in No 2 B D Company, in London was dispatched to the H Q of a Canadian Brigade, where he was told that one of their companies had taken over control of a large marshalling yard in Holland. In it was a train of eight trucks, loaded with component parts of the V2 Rocket. Up to that time, no complete rocket had been recovered and so it was imperative that these were able to be sent back to the U.K. for research. Unfortunately, the whole train was booby trapped !

When he got to the site, he found that each truck was wired to an explosive charge. The first and last truck had a 500kg bomb attached, linked to the whole explosive booby trap system. Each truck had a number of German demolition charges, which were contained in metal casings, threaded to take igniters. The whole lot was was connected up with trip wires and instantaneous fuze wire.

There were two types of igniters fitted. One would explode if the trip wire was cut and the other would work if the trip wire was stretched. Thus, if one cut a taut wire, the whole lot would explode or if, unfortunately, one tripped over a loose wire, the effect would be the same. This was the job given to Sgt Brinton.

He was able to make all the igniters safe, apart from those in the two 500kg bombs, which still presented a threat. But these he, subsequently, dealt with.

The Canadian Brigade Commander was delighted with his work and said he would commend him to his O.C. He heard nothing more ! Until, just after V.E. day, when he was serving in No 211 Field Park Company RE. in Germany, he received the British Empire Medal. Even today, he treasures the letter which accompanied the award. It read;-

Buckingham Palace

I greatly regret that I am unable to give you personally the award which you have so well earned.

I now send it to you with my congratulations and my best wishes for your future happiness.

GEORGE R I

29.10.1946

* * * * * * * * * * * *

Capt M R (Ferdy) Bool was posted to No 25 Bomb Disposal Company, in November 1941 and spent until August 1944 in the London area. The Company went to France on August 1st, which was fortunate as they had been bombed out of their quarters by flying bombs.

Their first base was in Caen, Major John Setchell was the Officer Commanding the Company. In the September the HQ moved to Brussels, whilst Ferdy spent his time clearing bombs in the Ghent, Bruges and Louvain area. The following April he was posted to HQ 1st Corps in Germany, as SORE 3 (Staff Officer, Royal Engineers, Grade 3). He writes; *"I thought that I had got a 'chairborne' job and I had left all my B D equipment in Belgium. Soon after I arrived the Chief Engineer came into my office and told me that there was an unexploded bomb beside the approach road to the Xanter bridge, which was one of the main supply routes for the 2nd Army. I tried, unsuccessfully, to contact Major Sharman, the O.C. No 24 Bomb Disposal Company, the only Company in the area.*

It thus fell to me to visit the site. I found the bomb, half buried by the side of the road with its tail visible. There was no sign of life, apart from a bulldozer clearing a way through the smoking ruins of the town. In desperation, I borrowed a monkey wrench from the driver and managed to remove the tail fuze. Some digging revealed the nose fuze, which also yielded to the persuasion of this all powerful tool.

I felt that my ration of luck must have used up for the rest of the war, was his comment after the event.

* * * * * * * * * * * *

Very little has been mentioned of the fact that many officers and Other Ranks of the Royal Engineers, were trained divers - by the Royal Navy of course - (The author was one of them,)

63 Port Construction and Repair Company RE were tasked with the job of clearing Dieppe harbour. Sapper T L Walker of that unit was in the first recce party to enter Dieppe. He located and removed underwater mines and demolition depth charges. At Flushing, by his efforts, six sunken vessels were raised and the first berths were cleared for shipping, in mine infested waters and in proximity to known delay action torpedoes

At Bergen-Op-Zoom, his persistence, under extremely adverse conditions enabled a large sunken dredger to be raised for operational requirements.

At Beveland he dived so often in mine and ice-packed waters that his hands and limbs became affected and ultimately he had to go to hospital.

For his persistently high standard of devotion of duty and courage in the face of silent and insidious enemy, performed under solitary and remote conditions, with the ever - present realisation that an accident or mistake would result in terrible death, he was awarded the George Medal.

* * * * * * * * * * * *

On the morning of 24th August 1944 an Allied air attack developed on the town of Brunswick, near to which was situated a Prisoner of War Camp, known as Oflag 79, containing some 2,600 officers and their batmen.

Twelve heavy bombs, some anti personnel and incendiary bombs fell inside the Camp compound. Three of the anti personnel bombs penetrated the roof of building known as House No 7, which accommodated 50 sick patients.

Captain J M (James) Ratcliffe of the Middlesex Regiment volunteered to remove the bombs to a safe place although he had had no previous experience in Bomb Disposal and it was not part of his normal duties to undertake such a task. He successfully removed all three bombs, with the aid of a bucket and put them in a place of safety and removed the detonators, rendering them harmless.

In addition to this act of conspicuous bravery he returned to the attic of House No 7 and succeeded in putting out three incendiary bombs.

The award of the George Medal was published in the London Gazette on 21st February 1946.

* * * * * * * * * * * *

Major Setchell, who had commanded 25 B D Company during the invasion. Was subsequently posted to command No 206 Works Section RE. In the August of 1944, Lt Gen Bernard Montgomery had his Tactical H Q at Blay, some 14 miles from Caen. Major Setchell was in Caen, which had been captured on 10th July, but the eastern suburbs were not cleared until 20th July. The Units' task had been to remove booby traps and some 'mine lifting', in addition to 'liberating' the furniture, cutlery, glassware - and a piano - from the German Officers Mess. The inhabitants had departed rather hastily, as food was found on the plates on the dining table.

In and around Caen were several thousand troops, both English and Canadian troops. The weather was hot and the troops were thirsty. The 'Official' ration was one beer per person per week ! Even that proved to be optimistic, as up to then, no one had even seen a bottle of beer.

It would appear that information of the existence of a Brewery at Fleury-sur-Orne, reached Major Setchell, who decided to reconnoitre the site. On arrival, it proved to be in a bit of a mess, in that all the buildings had suffered from shell and mortar fire. Not a window remained and most of the roof had been blown off. The first impression was that it was a complete ruin. In fact, on closer inspection the plant inside seemed to have suffered little damage.

No mains water was available and the generating station at Caen was out of action, no local power was available. However, he was keen to get the brewery going. A Major Lamb, who worked for the NAAFI/EFI had promised technical help and also would ensure the supply of Hops and Malt, etc, for the production. Obviously, the NAAFI would be very happy to have a local Brewery rather than having to get their supplies from the U.K. It was agreed that 'IF' the plant could actually produce a beer, then they would go ahead. It was to be kept 'VERY SECRET', otherwise representatives of all local units would be queueing up outside the Brewery.

A Sgt Bolton was appointed O.C. Brewery and sworn to silence. He had been a butcher before the war, but had had experience in the supervision of a large operation.

We learnt that the Head Brewer had been shot by the Germans, but soon after a former Brewery foreman appeared and was of considerable help thereafter.

Water was a problem, but being Royal Engineers, sufficient piping was found - about half a mile - along with filters, diesel generators, and with a supply of coal, courtesy of the RASC. (Royal Army Service Corps) - REME (Royal Electrical & Mechanical Engineers) made and gave us various fittings, mainly for the bottling plant, but were not told as to their actual use !

After three or four weeks, It was reported to Major Lamb, that they were in a position to go into production and that were ready to receive supplies.

On 25th August, Paris fell and about two weeks later Major Lamb rushed into the office to say that he had been posted as O.C. Paris hotels and was on his way.

During September work progressed on the plant in the Brewery and by the beginning of October it was agreed that sufficient progress had been made to make a 'Trial Brew'. It was a disaster - a typical 'wishy washy' French beer. It was realised that an 'Expert' was needed.

I was fortunate, in that a fellow officer on the Chief Engineers Staff came from an English Brewery family. I invited him over for lunch and explained my predicament to a very surprised Staff Officer. Who agreed to help, providing he had a few 'samples' to test ! The advice brought a quick improvement and the next brew was more than just 'acceptable'. Two crates were sent to the staff officer.

With the departure of Major Lamb, there was no sign that the NAAFI were remotely interested. On site there was now a stock of hops and malt, which was estimated at being at least sufficient for a year's production. They were in a position to produce beer with no buyers, apart from another brewery about 150 miles away. However, things were about to change. Now that the Germans had been pushed well back towards their own country, Brig Montgomery, decided that there should be three Clubs in Caen for the troops, an Officers Club, one for W.O's & Sgts and an Other Ranks Club. These were 'Officially' supplied by the NAAFI, but only with soft drinks.

It was then I decided to confess to our operation and I told Capt Bill Morgan who was the 'Q' on the Brigadiers staff of our operation - giving him a sample ! He quietly arranged for several hundred cases of beer to be delivered to the OR's Club.

Brigadier Montgomery opened the Club and ended his speech with the regret that the NAAFI could only supply soft drinks, only to be presented with a glass of foaming beer. Other Clubs were so supplied once they had opened, but no one knew of the source. All orders for beer had to go through 'official' R E channels. We even had to put on extra shifts to supply the Christmas rush.

In February 1945 my Company was ordered forward and I had to give up my Brewery. I phoned the CRE to tell him that he had inherited a Brewery which had been supplying his Mess for some months.

Major Setchell has the last words on this episode by saying; *"It is well known that Sappers can turn their hands to most things, but I would be surprised to learn of any Sapper Officer who managed to run a Brewery, concurrently with his other duties"*

* * * * * * * * * * * *

In the early hours of Sunday 22nd April 1945, two 'Light' Platoons from No 6 B D Company sailed for France, arriving at Boulogne a few hours later. They were 'billeted' at Marquise, about half way between Boulogne and Calais, in buildings which had previously been occupied by a German Signals unit. Their first tasks were to demolish three 16 inch guns at Sandgatte, four 11 inch guns at Framzelle and a V3 site at Mimoeques.

The gun emplacements were demolished using, in the main, their own shells. The Platoons certainly did not carry sufficient explosives to blow up such strong concrete structures - and the shells were there, anyway !

The destruction of the concrete roof of the V3 site proved interesting, to those involved, and somewhat experimental. It was 235 ft long and some 100 ft wide, with a thickness of up to 17 ft 6 inches.

'Beehive' charges were used. (These were a specially designed *shaped* charge, which would direct the full force of the explosion in one direction, rather like a current laser beam.) They were stacked in three's and placed at six feet intervals across the width and fired simultaneously. Each explosion produced a two inch diameter hole, right through the slab. These were then filled with explosive. This resulted in the slab being cut in half, just like cutting a piece of cheese.

An 11 inch gun emplacement at Framzelle, one mile South of Cap Griz Nez, opposite Dover. Demolished 19th June 1945.

198

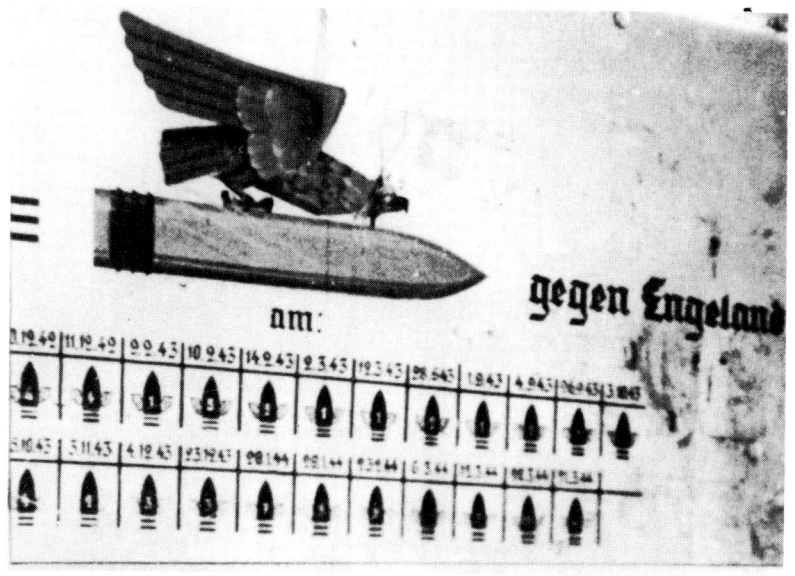

A painting on the wall of a gun emplacement at Framzelle, showing the dates on which shells were fired at Dover and Folkestone.

Inside the magazine of the gun emplacement. Some of these shells were used to effect the demolition of the site.

199

The actual moment of demolition of the gun emplacement at Framzelle.

A close up of the result of the demolition.

A V3 site at Mimoeques, Pas de Calais. The concrete slab contained exit ports for the V3 rocket barrels (never finished). The damage was caused by a 12,000lb 'Tallboy' bomb, dropped by Group Capt L Cheshire VC on 6th July 1944.
All photos courtesy of Capt C Walker.

Chapter Eighteen

1945

Along with about fifteen other officers, Lieut E E (Eric) Wakeling, of No 14 B D Company, was sent on No 5A 'Special Diving and B.D. Refresher Course' at Ripon in January 1945 - Even qualifying as a Diver, in the old Seibe Gorman suit. Others will probably remember the water tank where they did their 'Basic Diving Training'. They used to watch, every morning, whilst the Royal Navy personnel broke the ice ! Put in a steam hose - and a thermometer - when it read 38f, They were in !

One of the jobs included cutting through a steel hawser, with a hacksaw. Lieut Wakeling says " *Whilst I was cutting I began wondering why the water was turning red. - I was sawing through my thumb - And I didn't feel a thing!!" It was also quite a strange experience to see the sawdust rising when one was sawing a plank of wood.*

He further quotes;- "*The 'Booby Trapping' part of the course was the best ! We were split into groups. Each group booby trapped a building, then had to 'delouse' a building that another group had set up. On the last day some of us kept the various mechanisms which we recovered - 'L' delays, release mechanisms etc., Taking them back to our quarters where we proceeded to booby trap each others rooms. - I had an 'L' delay under my bed which went off at 03.00 hrs. I put a release mechanism under my boots, which went off when the 'Batwoman' picked them up. - She came back later, whilst I was*

*having dinner and sewed up the arms and legs of my
pyjamas !"*

* * * * * * * * * * * * *

On Feb 7th L/Sgt Edwards and Spr Cooper, of No
14 B D Company, were killed in a coastal minefield at
Filey.

On 19th the O.C. Major I (Ivor) Powell,
accompanied by Lieut E Wakeling went to Eastern
Command HQ, to discuss the proposed move of part of
the Company to Shoreham, Sussex for new duties.

On 25th the HQ of No 14 B D Company and an
Advance Party, moved from Leeds to Shoreham. In
addition to the O.C. Lieut George Churchill also moved to
Shoreham. All other officers, including the 2IC, with their
sections came under the command of the O.C. No 1 B D
Company. On 27th March, the responsibility of all UXB's
in the Region were handed over to No 1 B D Company,
which were based in Newcastle.

On 27th/28th, two Sections of the Company,
commanded by Lieuts John Walsh and Eric Wakeling
moved to Shoreham by road.

Capt Charles Cann, already mentioned, when
awarded the George Medal whilst still a Sgt was posted in
as 2IC Company. Lieut C V (Charles) Sadler and Lieut T
(Birty) Birtwhistle, who commanded sections already
involved in minefield clearance in the area were 'posted in'
to the Company.

Lieut Charles Sadler had already been there since
early 1942, engaged on UXB's and later on minefield
clearance along the South coast from Worthing to
Dungeness. Plus the removal of a crashed aircraft on the
shingle there. Whilst Lieut Birtwhistle and his section had
been working with Capt Cann on the 'Experimental
Jetting' side.

The Company's new duties were to develop a High
Pressure Water Jetting system for the clearance of mines

in shingle which, up to then had accounted for a higher than average deaths during minefield clearance. Having developed the equipment and system, they were then tasked with training teams from all Bomb Disposal Companies, currently involved in coastal minefield clearance of shingle beaches.

On 20th May, two crews from Nos 4 and 12 B D Companies arrived for their training in High Pressure Water Jetting. At the end of the two weeks course, they were issued with their vehicles and equipment and took them back to their units. That day, two more crews, from Nos 11 and 16 B D Companies arrived. From then on, every two weeks, two more crews arrived, were trained and issued with their equipment. By 26th August all the crews had been trained and all units had the equipment necessary for clearing minefields in shingle.

Unfortunately, on July 31st Capt Charles Cann died in hospital, whilst on the operating table for the minor operation of a tonsillectomy.

* * * * * * * * * * * *

By April 1945, Lieut William (Bill) Borthwick of No 11 B D Company had been engaged on minefield clearance for about a year and had already cleared in the region of 1,600 mines.

On 27th April, whilst he was working on a minefield South of Dunbar, he received a message that there had been an accident in another minefield North of the town. When he got there he found that two mines had exploded and that three Prisoners of War had been killed and a further nine were injured and were still lying in the minefield.

Lieut Borthwick and his Sgt swept a passage into the minefield, recovered the wounded and their dead colleagues. This was difficult, as most of them did not speak English and tended to move about when they saw the stretcher parties coming. There was a possibility that anyone of them could have trodden on a mine and killed their rescuers.

He was unfortunate enough to receive another similar message later in the year that there had been an accident in the Peffer Sands minefield. This time there were four dead bodies to recover.

'Bill' was awarded the George Medal for *"Operating, at great personal risk, in a situation fraught with difficulties and by his own initiative and gallant act, ensured that the wounded men were recovered with greatest possible speed and sent to hospital"*

Sgt Harold Craik was awarded the BEM for his bravery at the Dunbar operation.

* * * * * * * * * * * *

By a coincidence, another George Medal was awarded to an officer of No 11 B D Company, for his bravery on the minefields. - Dunbar being mentioned. - A citation reads;- "A minefield located near Dunbar proved difficult and dangerous to clear of mines owing to the unexpected reaction of the rocks on mine detectors. On 14th September an accident occurred at this minefield and the officer in charge and three men being killed." *Another officer removed the bodies.*

The minefield was wired up. The morale of the men involved being badly shaken by the accident.

However, it was still necessary to clear the minefield, although it was known to be a difficult and hazardous operation, since the remaining mines were in a rocky area and the mine detectors were known to be unreliable under such circumstances.

On 27th Sept Capt Briggs took a party back to the minefield and, alone, in view of his men, located and disarmed several mines. He fully appreciated the dangers he was facing, but realising the urgency of the task and the need to restore the confidence of his men, he never faltered, thus setting a fine example of courage and devotion to duty. As a result the men subsequently turned to their task with confidence and determination and the minefield was cleared without further accident.

* * * * * * * * * * * *

At that time, No 11 B D Company was very busy with minefield problems. During a heavy storm a portion of the minefield at Fergus, North of Aberdeen, collapsed into the sea. Two of the mines were left on the face of the cliff, held by the wires which connected the mines together when they were laid. Lieut Walter Brown went to the minefield, when it was reported, to find a very dangerous situation. He decided that he would personally deal with the two mines on the cliff face and crawled down a very unstable soil, successfully disarming both mines. He then disarmed another twelve mines which were on the edge of the cliff which was liable to collapse at any minute.

There was also the possibility that if a mine moved it would detonate and cause sympathetic detonation of other mines in the field.

But for his gallant action, carried out at great personal risk, there was considerable danger that the minefield might have collapsed, creating a situation of extreme danger, particularly for those who would have to follow to disarm them.

* * * * * * * * * * * *

In October 1945, a 250kg bomb was discovered at Belmont Road, Belfast, adjacent to the Automatic Telephone Exchange serving the Northern Ireland Parliament at Stormont and two other government buildings.

The bomb was found to be fitted with (17) and (50) fuzes. The (50) was immunised, but it was found necessary to move the bomb away from the site with the (17) fuze stopped by the magnetic clockstopper. There was always a risk that the bomb would explode if the (17) was removed.

Unfortunately, in transit the clockstopper was damaged, rendering the remainder of the operation extremely dangerous. However, it was successfully removed to an area where it could be blown up without doing any damage.

The speed with which he had dealt with the bomb allowed a large number of people who had been evacuated at very short notice, to return to their homes before nightfall.

Both Lieut John Deacon and Sgt Alfred Parker, who assisted him throughout, were awarded George Medals.

* * * * * * * * * * * *

Sapper Gerald Fielding tells of a 1400kg bomb he worked on. It had fallen just off the main road between Beaconscot and Chalfont St Giles in Buckinghamshire. *"We were halfway between four cottages and a mansion, near Amersham. I was the Duty Driver and with the three tonner I had to tow a bomb up to the mansion. The elderly gentleman who lived there had bought it off the War Office ! He had it placed in front of the mansion and charged the public a shilling a time to look at it. All the money he collected he gave to Dr Barnardo's Home."*

* * * * * * * * * * * *

The following photographs show the amount of time and effort that often had to be applied to achieve a successful result.

The bomb, in this case is an S.C. 1,000kg, commonly known as 'Herman' after the fat leader of the Luftwaffe, Herman Goering.

From the first photograph it can be seen that the bomb 'misbehaved' itself, in that it did not follow the normal pattern of travelling in a straight line once it had entered the ground. As a result some tunnelling was required. Fortunately, chalk is very stable and unlikely to collapse suddenly, thus the shaft had the minium amount of timbering and the 'tunnel' was not supported. Mind you, there was not a lot of room in the tunnel, just enough to find the fuze and allow room to get to it and immunize it.

The officer is examining the fuze, to identify it before applying the appropriate immunising method.

Photo courtesy of Sgt O A Kent.

Having immunized and removed the fuze, the bomb is hauled out of the shaft. This was preferable to hand hauling it out, using shear legs, particularly with this size of bomb.

Quite often, the contents of the bomb was removed before taking it away from the site. The fuze can be seen in the foreground, to the left of the officer's hat. The 'base plate' or 'filler cap' can be seen further to the left.

Both photos courtesy of Sgt O A Kent.

Chapter Nineteen

CHANNEL ISLANDS

The Channel Islands, which, geographically, have a closer affinity to France rather than the U.K., have the unique claim of being the only British Territory occupied by German Forces during the war.

With Alderney only seven miles from the French coastline and Jersey just 14, they were within shelling distance and the British Government decided to 'demilitarise' them.

On June 20th 1940 all regular troops were withdrawn, but the German Government was not informed. For ten days the Germans tried to establish whether the Islands would be defended, or not.

Reconnaissance flights over the Islands by the Luftwaffe were unable to clarify the situation - and there were no 'White Flags' flying.

On 28th June, the Germans decided to carry out an 'Armed Reconnaissance' over Jersey and Guernsey. Unfortunately, the evacuation of some 17,000 islanders was misconstrued by the German High Command as 'Troop Movements'. This resulted in some 180 bombs being dropped on harbour installations of both St Helier and St Peter Port, killing some 44 civilians and causing much destruction.

Whilst the invasion troops were being assembled at Cherbourg, the pilot of a Dornier DO17, who had been flying a reconnaissance mission over Guernsey, noted that there was no visible activity around the airfield and decided to land, only to find that it was completely deserted.

He returned to Cherbourg and informed Admiral Lindau that the island was undefended and the immediate occupation was ordered. The invasion by sea was cancelled and the Germany Navy 'flew' in, the following day, 1st July 1940.

In June 1941, when the Germans invaded Russia, Hitler was fearful of the British recovering the Islands and so the defences had to be strengthened.

On the Contentin Peninsular General Marcke had five divisions under his command. One Division, the 319 Infantry, with 36,000 men was moved to the Islands.

The Defence Plan was to have 200 'strong points' on the two main islands. Heavy Coastal Batteries were to be installed along with the laying of minefields and possible sea landing area defended by the installation of under water obstacles plus mined tetrahedra. 'Roll bombs' were installed on cliff tops. Flame throwers at road junctions and anti aerial landing defences, consisting of poles erected in possible landing areas, with French 300lb shells attached.

16,000 foreign workers were imported, mainly from Russia and Poland, to dig tunnels, bunkers and gun emplacements.

Between 27th October 1941 and 23rd March 1945, some 72,566 mines were laid in 115 minefields. The whole idea was to make the Island an impregnable fortress.

* * * * * * * * * * * *

Following the invasion of France in June 1944, plans were laid to put an invasion force on both islands. A Task Force of some 6,000 men was formed and named 'Force 135'. The Operation was code named 'Nestegg',

210

whilst those given to the invasion of Jersey and Guernsey were 'Booty' and 'Agent' respectively.

* * * * * * * * * * * *

In 1943 Lieut H W (Harry) Beckingham was with the author in No 14 B D Company. The latter was Best Man at Harry's wedding. He was posted to Command No 24 B D Platoon in September 1944. The Platoon became the Bomb Disposal element of Force 135. Although formed in September 1944, it was not until 11th May 1945 that they sailed from Plymouth.

Whilst waiting he spent most of his time clearing the minefields along the Devon and Dorset coasts.

It was not until 3rd May 1941 that Operation 'Nestegg' was activated. On 5th May a radio message was broadcast to the Islands that the GOC Southern Command was authorised to receive the unconditional surrender of the German occupying forces.

It was not until 9th May that the document was signed, on the quarter deck of HMS Bulldog.

By this time, Lt Harry Beckingham had an increased establishment, now consisting of one Sgt, two L/Sgts, 6 Cpls, 8 L/Cpls, 28 Sappers and one ACC cook. He had to split his platoon into two. Half going to Guernsey, under the command of his Sgt, whilst the other half, under his command went to Jersey.

His first impression was the depth and strength of the fortifications. The Germans had completed all their plans for the defence of the islands, which left him with one hell of a job to clear and render safe all installations.

His first job was to go to the 'Pomme d'Or' Hotel in St Helier, which was the the German Naval Headquarters, to take the German Force Commander a prisoner of war. Kapitan von Kleve was duly handed over to a Military Police escort and taken to a landing craft in the bay.

His next job was to check the hotel for mines and booby traps, before declaring it safe for the occupancy of Colonel Robinson with his Tactical Headquarters

For the following two days he toured the island, checking up on all the mined defences. Firstly, he and his men *disposed of* a large quantity of gelignite which was stored in Fort Regent but had become very unstable and dangerous to all and sundry.

Slipways were also rapidly cleared to allow local fisherman access to the sea.

To assist him with the job he had 300 P.O.W's (Prisoners of War) with a German officer and a bilingual German soldier to act as interpreter. The job of 'minefield clearance' was soon broken down into various categories. The Germans had not just laid coastal minefields, but had mined all fields which could have been Glider landing grounds. The Tetrahedra on the shore were also mined and in addition they were tasked with the removal of all the barbed wire.

Working twelve hours a day, seven days a week, an average of 1,000 mines were lifted each day and by 25th May some 4,100 *schu* mines and 600 *Tellermines* had been lifted from around the perimeter of the airfield. Throughout June and July they were averaging some 1,500 mines a day. They also recovered a British 500lb bomb. Lieut Beckingham was unfortunate, in that one occasion, where he had discovered that the mines in one particular field were very sensitive, he decided to blow up each mine individually. It was unfortunate, because when the first one was blown up, it caused a 'sympathetic' detonation of the whole minefield, from the detonation of just that one mine. It caused considerable damage and some shock to the local residents. The explosion partially demolished a nearby house. The lady occupant told him later; *"Don't worry, you have got rid of the Germans, now the mines, so we can now rebuild our lives and live in peace."*

There were, in fact 72,886 mines laid in Guernsey, but the Germans had lifted 6110 mines in 1944. Some credit is due to the Germans, who had made and kept very accurate maps of each of the 94 minefields they had laid, which no doubt, saved a lot of lives.

Whilst the minefield clearance was going on, the Tellermines which had been fitted to the Tetrahedra, were removed and the 'possible' glider landing grounds had their poles and booby traps removed and the fields were returned to their owners. Much of all the hardware, such as the poles, barbed wire and any other defences were taken to a quarry and dumped.

A further three German bombs, this time each of 250 kg, which had been dropped prior to the German invasion of the island, were recovered and defused. The Germans had just left them, for five years, without a thought for the safety of the local residents.

The underwater obstacles were the worst to deal with, being made of steel girders, to which 300lb French shells had been wired. Even at the lowest Spring Tide, they were still underwater. Defusing meant having to don a diving suit before going down to do the work.

The Germans were very inventive, when it came to using up captured French munitions - They had already used some French incendiaries in their 50kg aerial bombs (Sprengbrand C 50) - Here on the islands, they used French shells, along with the poles in the fields. 300lb shells were stood on their bases with fuzes fitted in the nose and they were wired together, like a spiders web. In some instances the shells were buried some six foot from a pole but, again, connected with a wire. Even the New Pier at St Peter Port had a 300lb shell affixed to each support - some 198 shells needed to be defuzed.

They also invented the 'Roll Bomb'. Again, using one thousand 300lb French shells, which were laid on top of the cliffs, tied to a picket. An igniter was put in the nose of the shell which was wired to another picket. If there had been a landing, the shell would have been released from the first picket and rolled down the cliff. The wire attached to the second picket would activate the igniter and the bomb would explode when it was some way down the cliff.

The majority of the clearance was completed by 25th July 1945. However, working at such a pace, casualties were inevitable and six Germans were killed, whilst some 14 were injured, some seriously.

* * * * * * * * * * * *

In 1946 Capt C V (Charles) Sadler, who was attached to No 16 B D Company was posted to the Channel Island of Alderney, to join Capt J C (John) Hunt MBE, where they followed the footsteps of Lieut Beckingham on Jersey and Guernsey, (In 1945) defusing French 300lb bombs which had been attached to poles on possible glider landing grounds. He writes; "*There were poles in the fields to which were attached buried 50kg bombs, to blow up incoming aircraft. The field adjoined a minefield of Tellermines, laid in tandem with 'pull igniters' between each pair. To add to the 'Disposers' problem they had been wrapped in barbed wire before being buried and armed.*

* * * * * * * * * * * *

The 'Pomme D'OR Hotel' St Helier, Jersey, the German Naval H.Q.

The Jetty at St Peter Port, set up for demolition in case of invasion.
The shells were 300lb, captured from the French.
Both photos courtesy of Capt H W Beckingham.

An S.C. 1000kg bomb being recovered from a shaft on the 'Meads', near the railway station at Bishops Stortford. The digging was in chalk, but a nearby Artesian well filled the shaft every night, thus requiring sheet steel piling to prevent the shaft from collapsing. It can be seen that this was a major engineering job.
Photo courtesy of Lt Col P S Wadsworth.

Chapter Twenty

POST WAR

On February 28th 1946, No 14 B D Company was disbanded. Major Ivor Powell went to No 6 B D Company at Bristol. Capt Eric Wakeling was posted to 20 B D Company at Sevenoaks, whilst Lieut George Churchill was posted to the HQ of No 12 B D Company at Horsham and Lieuts Birtwhistle and Sadler remained where they were and also came under the control of the same Company. Two weeks later Capt Eric Wakeling was posted to No 12 B D Company as their 2IC.

This set up was to last less than four months, as No 12 B D Company was disbanded on 15th June and we all dispersed. Major Goodman to another Company where the O.C. had been demobbed, Lieut George Churchill to MEXE (The Military Experimental Establishment at Christchurch) where, unfortunately, he died from an accident with detonators later that year, having just got engaged.

Capt Eric Wakeling went to No 2 B D Company in London as a D.O.B.D. (District Officer Bomb Disposal).

One day when he was the only officer at the unit, a reporter arrived from the Evening News. The reporter wanted a story about the number of unexploded bombs still in London. He was taken into the 'Ops room', where he was shown a map of the remaining UXB's - some 52. That evening the paper ran a banner headline '52 Unexploded Bombs still in London'. Subsequently, Capt

Wakeling was asked to appear on the BBC. His contract read "52 *Unexpected* bombs in London".

In 1996 the Daily Telegraph ran two articles on the subject of unexploded missiles in London. There were then 162. This was followed by, yet another BBC program which involved the author.

* * * * * * * * * * * *

A wartime bomb which fell in a field at Coleshill in Buckinghamshire was not discovered until June 1946, when it was reported to the authorities. 22 B.D Section were detailed for the work of excavating the bomb. It was found at a depth of 38 feet, immunised and brought safely to the surface.

* * * * * * * * * * * *

Spr Fielding (extreme right) stands with the crew from No 22 B D Section, which had just recovered a 1400kg semi armour bomb.
Photo courtesy of Spr G Fielding

The 'Congleton Chronicle' dated Friday 9th May 1947, had a front page story of a bomb in a field at Bunts Lane Farm, Marton. Whether it was the fact that it was now two years after the war's end or that German Prisoners of War were being used to dig up bombs is a matter of conjecture.

Sapper Fielding, previously mentioned, had now moved to Huyton, Liverpool and had been working on a small bomb, just outside Bury. His section took on this job as soon as the Bury job was finished. At first the soil was good to dig, but after about six feet they came across water and it required two pumps, working 24 hours a day to keep it under control. After three months of digging the bomb was found at a depth of 25 feet. It proved to be an S.C. 250kg bomb.

* * * * * * * * * * * *

Lieut C V (Charles) Sadler was still working the Sussex Coast, clearing the minefields, when he received a call for assistance, from the Royal Navy. Apparently, a Sea Mine had been washed up on the shore at Hove, right opposite a hotel, which had just been refurbished, following its employment during the war as a Royal Navy Shore Station, HMS King Alfred.

The Royal Navy did not have sufficient men or equipment to deal with the mine and the Army was asked to remove it.

Lieut Sadler relates; "*Sgt Hayes and I got to the site about 09.00hrs, when the tide was out. Nearby roads had been closed and the whole area had been evacuated.*

The mine was mostly covered and well below High Water Mark. It was also waterlogged and I decided to try and blow it out of the shingle. Using condoms, filled with Ammonal as our 'lifting' explosive, we pushed about six of them down the side of the mine and connected them up electrically, retiring to an underground car park. I pressed down the exploder - Nothing Happened ! - We retraced our steps, checking the electric cable until we found a break some way down the beach. Mending it, we retired behind a groin, instead of returning to the car park, that was a mistake ! This time our Ammonal exploded, but so did the mine. We were very shaken when the groin almost disintegrated. Damage elsewhere was considerable. Windows in the King Alfred were blown out as were most along the sea front for a distance of half a mile either side of the hotel.

A Naval Captain came storming down the beach and I told him firmly that, from the start, I had told Commander Riley.

    a) What I had intended to do.
    b) That it was at his request.
    c) That it was done with his approval and
    d) That it was HIS responsibility.

Some days later I got an order to attend a Naval inquiry at Portsmouth. I repeated my proviso that I had given Commander Riley and said I had no intention of attending their inquiry. That was the last I heard of it."

* * * * * * * * * * * *

Later in the year Lieut Sadler was back at Dungeness clearing the coastal minefields. He had had three sappers posted in, all of whom had been 'Chindits'. They did not mix very easily with the rest of the men in the Section as they considered that those in B D had had an 'easy' war. They even sat apart when eating their meal at the site.

There was another section, not under the command of Lieut Sadler nearby who, it appeared to him, were not observing the strict safety rules, when in a minefield. The inevitable happened and there was an accident. A number were blown up and bits of their bodies were distributed over a wide area, including the minefield in which his section was working. Walking around the area already cleared, he found a hand. At lunchtime he placed the hand on the table where the three sappers were sitting. In spite of their 'Chindit Toughness', they were all sick. After that, there was no 'isolation' and they became very good members of the Section.

* * * * * * * * * * * * *

Huyton, Liverpool, May 1947. A close up of the bomb shaft, showing the conditions under which men of No 9 B D Section had to work. Sheet steel piling and at least two large pumps were needed to keep the water level down to a manageable working condition

Members of No 9 B D Section with some German POW's, who assisted them in recovering an S.C. 500kg German bomb. Lieut Nickols is on the extreme right, whilst Spr Fielding is fourth from the left.
Both photos courtesy of Spr G Fielding

221

Finally, all the wartime B D Companies were disbanded, Nos 2, 7 and 16 being the last to go. There just remained an H.Q. B D Units (UK) based at Broadbridge Heath, near Horsham, which controlled two B D Troops, based at Whetstone Camp, North London and Fort Widley, on the hills overlooking Portsmouth.

Then in 1951 a new B D Regiment (No 137) was formed, with three Companies, now renamed Squadrons. This was quickly followed by 142 B D Regiment in the following year, with three Squadrons and 144 B D Regiment, also with three Squadrons, in 1953.

HQ B D Units moved to Lodge Hill, Rochester in 1966. apart from that move this remained the situation until 1967, when all three B D Regiments were disbanded on 31st March.

No 590 Specialist Team EOD (V) (Yet another name) was formed on 1st April.

In 1974 HQ B D Units was renamed 33 Engr Regt (EOD), and expanded to three squadrons, later to be increased to four. Then in 1988 a T.A. B D Regiment (No 101) was formed.

This is the 'Order of Battle' that exists at the time of the writing of this book. They have currently troops in Bosnia, the Falklands, Cyprus, Northern Ireland, in addition to their operational role in the U.K.

* * * * * * * * * * * *

Officers of No 137 B D Regiment at Broadbridge Heath, Summer 1952.
With Lieut Gen Tuck. CB. Engineer in Chief.
Photo courtesy of Col B S T Archer GC OBE ERD

Senior Bomb Disposal officers at their HQ, Broadbridge Heath, circa 1958.
Left to Right. Lt Col W G Parker MBE GM, C.O. 144 B D Regt, Lt Col N H S Barker,
C.O. HQ BD Units (UK), Lt Col P J Hands MBE, C.O. 137 B D Regt and Lt Col B S
T Archer GC, C.O. 142 B D Regt.

Senior officers of 142 B D Regt, at Broadbridge Heath, circa 1958
Left to Right. Major A. Blackwell, O.C. 290 B D Sqn, Major C H Green GM, 2IC
Regt. Lt Col B S T Archer GC, C.O. Regt, Major E E Wakeling, O.C. 547 B D Sqn,
Major L H Morgan GM, O.C. 550 B D Sqn.

224

Officers of No 142 B D Regiment at Broadbridge Heath, Summer 1966.
Back row (L–R) Capt G C Berry, Capt R F H Wilshaw, Lt P J North, Lt M J Martin, Capt D W Badby, Lt R A M Cook, Capt J F W Craddick, Lt B R Williams, Lt H L Wright, Capt A M C Bertuchi, Capt M J Herbert, 2/Lt R A Leigh, Capt I M McFadyen, Capt C J Lisle. Front row, Major M F Ingham, Major M J Inglis ERD, Col B S T Archer GC OBE ERD, Lt Col E E Wakeling ERD, Maj Gen Sir Gerald Duke KBE CB DSO, Engineer in Chief, Col W G Parker MBE GM ERD, Major A W Singer ERD, Major G E Wakeling.

Officers of No 144 B D Regiment, with the Hon Colonel, Col B S T Archer GC OBE, circa 1965
Front Row (L – R) Major W A French, ?, Col B S T Archer, Lt Col L H Morgan, Capt C Cowen, ?, ?,
Back Row, Lt Fenn, Capt J Best, Lt T H Panther, ?, Lt R F H Wilshaw, ?, Lt C J Miall, ?, Lt I R Berry, ?, Lt J Ford.
Photo courtesy of Col B S T Archer GC OBE ERD

In 1967, 590 Specialist Team, went to Penang for its Summer Camp. By now it was commanded by Major N P (Norman) Woollven. Their job was to assist a detachment of No 49 B D Sqn RE, a Regular Army unit, which was clearing the dumps of Japanese bombs. During their tour of two weeks (including travelling out there and back, they dealt with some 270 60kg bombs, plus one 250kg.

That year thousands of tons of bombs were dumped in the sea.

Major N P Woollven examines a partially uncovered 60kg Japanese bomb. He said; *"The bomb was leaking Picric acid, giving rise to Lead Picrate crystals, which are highly unstable."*
Photo courtesy of Major N P Woollven TD

Two sappers of 590 STRE EOD (V) recover a 60kg bomb. The working conditions can be seen as being atrocious and this was a Bomb Dump.
Photo courtesy of Major N P Woollven TD

The Commanding Officer, Lt Col E E Wakeling ERD inspecting the men of 142 B D Regiment RE at Old Park Barracks, Maidstone, 27th May 1966. He is followed by the O.C. 550 B D Sqn RE, Major M F Ingham, the 2IC Regt, Major A W Singer ERD and the Adjutant, Capt C J Lisle.

Appendix 'A'

GEORGE CROSSES AWARDED TO R.E. BOMB DISPOSAL PERSONNEL

Rank	Name	Date of London Gazette
Lt W L	ANDREWS	17 Sep 1940
2/Lt B S T	ARCHER	30 Sep 1941
Major H J L	BAREFOOT	22 Jan 1941
2/Lt M F	BLANEY	15 Apr 1941
L/Sgt W J	BUTTON	17 Sep 1940
2/Lt A F	CAMPBELL	22 Jan 1941
Lt R	DAVIES	30 Sep 1940
Sgt M	GIBSON	22 Jan 1941
Major C A J	MARTIN	11 Mar 1943
Lt Col A D	MERRIMAN	3 Dec 1940
Lt E W	REYNOLDS	7 Sep 1940
2/Lt E E	TALBOT	17 Sep 1940
Spr G C	WYLIE	30 Sep 1940

Appendix 'B'

GEORGE MEDALS AWARDED TO
R.E. BOMB DISPOSAL PERSONNEL

Rank and Name		DATE(LG)	LOCATION
Lt J G	ALLEN	5 May 44	Salerno
Sgt A J	ASHMORE	19 Nov 43	Grimsby
Sgt W H	BAILEY	10 Mar 44	Plymouth
Capt A G	BAINBRIDGE	30 Sept 41	London
2/Lt J	BARNES	22 Jan 41	Luton
Lt P A	BAYS	19 Oct 45	U.K.
Cpl W O	BEAN	17 Dec 40	Middleton
Capt A J	BIGGS	22 Jan 41	Birmingham
Lt T	BLACKSHAW	17 Aug 43	Mountnessing
Lt T W T	BLACKWELL MBE	6 Nov 42	Malta
Lt W S	BORTHWICK	28 Dec 45	Dunbar
Capt E L	BOURNE	23 Dec 43	Norfolk
Sgt J	BRABIN	15 Sept 44	Norfolk
Capt H	BRIGGS	9 Jul 46	Dunbar
Cpl C F	BRISTOW	17 Feb 42	Romford
Lt W M	BROWN	15 Mar 46	U.K.
Capt A G	BURNETT	1 Dec 44	English Channel
Lt F H	BUTLER	30 Sep 41	Clydebank
Sgt C M	CANN	22 Jan 41	Ipswich
Spr J W	CARTER	11 Mar 41	Gravesend
Spr S	CHESHER	17 Dec 40	U.K.
Sgt R J	CHESTER	28 Oct 41	Romford
Lt M A	CLINTON	17 Feb 42	Romford
Lt M A	CLINTON GM	17 Aug 43	Essex

Pl Offr	COOKE (H G)	11 Mar 41	Birmingham
Capt D W	CUNNINGTON	17 Dec 40	Weybridge
Lt C E	DAVIES	28 Oct 41	Weybridge
Capt J E	DEACON	25 Jun 46	Belfast
Lt T J	DEANE	17 Feb 42	Saxmundham
Lt R W	DEANS	11 Mar 43	Battersea
CQMS P N	DENISON	21 Oct 41	Sheffield
Capt W A	DIXON.MC	30 Sep 41	Holborn
Capt W A	FEATHER	28 Oct 41	Norwich/Norfolk
2/Lt J	FORD	11 Mar 41	Bexley
Capt S	GARSIDE	30 Sep 41	Barking
Lt G M	GAYLOR	20 Apr 45	Hassault
Lt L	GERHOLD	30 Sep 41	Clydebank
Major L	GERHOLD GM	17 Aug 43	Essex
Lt J H H	GRAY	10 May 44	Plymouth
Lt C H	GREEN	11 Mar 41	Gravesend
Capt H A	GROVER	30 Sep 41	Brentford
Sgt T	HALL	17 Aug 43	Essex
Lt E J	HALSTED-HANBY	22 Jan 41	Norwich
Lt P M	HENNINGS	2 Feb 45	East Coast
Capt E M	HEWITT	25 Mar 41	Tyneside
L/Sgt J H	HINTON	22 Jan 41	Coventry
Sgt L C	HOLLANDS	19 Nov 43	Grimsby
Cpl W	HONE	30 Sep 41	Coventry
Major J P	HUDSON MBE	20 Apr 43	London
Major J P	HUDSON MBE GM	15 Sep 44	Staplecross
Cpl F J	JACKSON	1 Dec 44	French Coast
Cpl J S	JELLEY	22 Jan 41	Norwich
Lt G M	JENSEN	19 Nov 43	Grimsby
Cpl W	JONES	2 Feb 45	Orbois (France)
Sgt W A	JONES	17 Dec 40	U.K.
Sgt E	LAING	30 Sep 41	Birmingham
Lt K	LANHAM	5 May 44	Taranto (Italy)
Spr B M	LAWSON	22 Jan 41	Norwich

Capt C W	LEA	30 Sep 41	Bromley
2/Lt R H	LEE	22 Jan 41	Birmingham
Capt J R	McCARTNEY	22 Jan 41	Hartshorne
Lt R C B	MAITLAND	24 Mar 42	Southampton
2/LtH A	MANSER	17 DEc 40	U.K
2/Lt F R	MARTIN	17 Dec 40	Chevening
Lt L C	MEYNELL	30 Sep 41	Coventry
Capt H	MITCHELL	17 Dec 40	U.K
Lt L H	MORGAN	5 Oct 45	Wyke Regis
Lt S N	NEWITT	24 Mar 42	London
Sgt A	PARKER	25 Jun 46	Belfast
L/Sgt R C	PARKER	27 May 41	Malta
Maj W G	PARKER MBE	5 Oct 45	Corsham
Lt B H P	PRICE	28 Oct 41	Plymouth
Sgt G H	QUARENDON	24 Mar 42	Hull
Lt E R	RABY	17 Dec 40	Manchester
Lt F	RADFORD	22 Jul 41	East Anglia
Lt D H	RAMAGE	11 Feb 41	St Helen's
Lt D S F	RAYNER	22 Jan 41	Birmingham
L/Sgt J B	RENFREW	19 Nov 43	Grimsby
Lt B L	RICHARDS	8 Jul 41	London
Lt K H	ROBINSON	28 Jul 44	Norwich
Lt H C	RUTH	13 Jan 42	Hull
L/Sgt A	SANDERS	30 Sep 41	Birmingham
Capt T H	SHARMAN	30 Sep 41	Birmingham
Lt R	SHARP	19 Nov 43	Grimsby
Capt C P	SHELBOURNE	22 Jul 41	Essex
Sgt C	SIMPSON	19 Nov 43	Grimsby
Lt E W	SIVIL	2 Feb 45	Sussex
CSM F	SMITH	21 Oct 41	Sunderland
Capt C C	STEWART	30 Sep 41	Kingston
L/Cpl E	SUTTLE	30 Sep 41	Coventry
Lt W C	SWINSON	15 Sep 44	Suffolk

Lt L N	TAYLOR	22 Jul 41	Tilbury
Sgt T	TAYLOR	10 Mar 42	Essex
Lt A C	THOMAS	19 Nov 43	Grimsby
Sgt E J	THORNE	17 Dec 40	UK
Lt R G	WALKER	2 Feb 45	France
Spr T L	WALKER	9 Nov 45	Dieppe/Flushing
Lt J P	WALTON	28 Oct 41	S E London/Kent
Sgt G A	WARDROPE	24 Mar 42	S E London
Lt J	WARREN	25 Aug 44	Kent
Capt A B	WATERS	10 Nov 44	UK
L/Sgt F	WHITE	2 Feb 45	Brighton
Capt D A	WILKINSON	17 Feb 42	Slough/Eton
Spr J	WILLIAMS	11 Mar 41	Lyndhurst
Sgt T J	WILLIAMS	28 Oct 41	Norwich
L C R	WOOD	11 Mar 41	Lyndhurst
Lt R A J	WOODS	24 Aug 45	Dorset

Appendix 'C'

WARTIME DOGGEREL by G R Ovens

I was posted to London in nineteen forty
to command a Bomb Disposal platoon
There was little delay to my first sortie
I hadn't expected hectic action so soon

Although *au fait* with explosives, as such
my knowledge of bombs was not great
I hope I would soon develop the touch
to work as safely as circumstances dictate

The excavation was already completed
the bomb exposed on one side
the other personnel had already retreated
and left me the next move to decide

236

I climbed down a bomb hole pit
gently I cleaned the fuze face
I was greatly relieved I must admit
to find the number was 15 (Commonplace)

Carefully I moved my spanner measure
to engage the lugs of the locking rings
if they moved without undue pressure
I knew I would be on top of things

The rings unscrewed without trouble
the fuze then could be lifted
I slid it out with scarcely a wobble
the bomb could soon be shifted.

Appendix 'D'

BOMB DISPOSAL SAPPERS LAMENT

We are the R.E. Bomb Disposers, enlisted for the war
and for many months we lay about 'til life became a bore.
The Jerry came along one day to break our sweet repose.
We now go round from place to place, his dud ones to
dispose.
Some people think they're funny and dropped for fun
but there's nothing ruddy funny about the Nazi Hun.
We have to get up early to thwart Adolf's little tricks,
to find out which are acid ones from those whose
clockwork ticks.
And if we get them out alright we do a little grin.
But if we don't...that's just too bad, they just inform our
next of kin.

Written by a Sapper of No 9 Bomb Disposal Company, RE. (Birmingham/Coventry)
WW II. circa 1940/41

Appendix 'E'

END OF COURSE EXAMINATION

The following is the examination paper set by the R.A.F. (Melksham) at the end of the course they ran for Army Bomb Disposal Officers in the early days of 1940.

<u>No 12 S, of T.T. Melksham</u>

<u>Bomb Disposal Course.</u>

<u>WRITTEN EXAMINATION</u>

Officers to attempt all questions.
Sergeants to attempt nine questions.

<u>Time allowed;-</u> _____ <u>3 hours.</u>

1.   Enumerate the various items which would receive your attention in making the reconnaissance of a reported unexploded bomb.
2.   Describe the operation of the Rheinmetall Fuze No. 15. What is the purpose of the various intervals and delays in it's timing ?
3.   Describe methods of protection against damage caused by the explosion of delay-action bombs, and state in what circumstances each would be used.
4.   What is a camouflet ? What factors would help you detect one ?
5.   A bomb has fallen into marshy ground adjoining an

important factory. What precautions would you take during the excavation to make work easier and safer for your men ?

6.   What action would you take with the following bombs, all priority "A"; if you found;-

  (a) A No. 15 fuze which had jammed.
  (b) A fuze of a new type.
  (c) A fuze which has had it's marking erased.
  (d) A fuze on the underside of the bomb.
  (e) A 28 B6 fuze in which both plungers are depressed.

  Would your actions be different if the bombs were priority "C". If so, how ?

7.   A 250kg has been uncovered at the depth of 18 feet in open fields. Timbering has been necessary during the excavation. You decide to demolish the bomb in situ. State what stores you would require, and give your procedure in detail.

8.   Enumerate sequence of use of the following equipment in dealing with a bomb with both a 17 and 50 fuze. Category "A.1." ready for handling, 6hrs after it had been dropped, stating items you would require on the spot, and state items listed here not required.

  (a) Sterilizer
  (b) Magnetic Clock Stopper No II
  (c) Plug Discharger
  (d) Fuze Extractor No II
  (e) Fuze Discharger Liquid
  (f) Stethoscope

9.   On reconnaissance you find an estimated 250kg. This bomb is in an Armament factory employing 1000 hands. State what action you would take, bearing in mind that you do not know what fuzes are in the bomb.

10.   What is the correct method of treating all fuzes except one before moving the bomb. Name the fuze to which this method does not apply.

What we know now is that, even if you didn't pass, you still went back to your unit as a 'Trained' B.D. Officer !

Appendix 'F'

THE BOMB DISPOSAL
SILVER CENTREPIECE

During 1960 it became clear that the emphasis in Bomb Disposal was changing from the disposal of conventional bombs towards the disposal of guided weapons. Clearly the time had come to commemorate in some way the gallantry of all ranks of the Corps of Royal Engineers, who had distinguished themselves in this exceptionally hazardous and unpleasant form of warfare - the disposal of the unexploded bomb, commonly known as the UXB.

The UXB was a menace which had never been imagined prior to 1940. It might be unexploded by deliberate design of the enemy or by accident. Either way it was a hazard to morale, life and property, and had to be removed. Because bombs buried themselves deep in the earth, under foundations, by railways, in factory floors and similar difficult places, only the Royal Engineers had the combination of Civil, Mechanical and explosive engineering knowledge to deal with them.

The cost was high, 246 officers and men lost their lives and to this must be added another 151 who were killed clearing our own minefields. Twelve George Crosses and countless other decorations were earned. The casualty rate was nearly two killed to one wounded.

The Bomb Disposal Unit (UK) RE therefore decided to commemorate these operations by a silver centrepiece for it's Officers Mess. A Committee was formed to raise funds and arrange for it's design and completion. The members of the committee were:-

Chairman. Brigadier H H Bateman CBE DSO MC
(A wartime Director of Bomb Disposal)
Colonel W G Parker MBE GM ERD
(Hon Col, B D Regts)
Lt Col B S T Archer GC OBE ERD RE
(O C 142 B D Regt RE)
Lt Col J H Clark MC RE
(O C B D Units (UK) RE)

Secretaries.
Major A B Hartley MBE GM RE (Until retired)
Major R H Hough MBE GM RE

Donations from serving and retired Bomb Disposal Officers came in quickly and a further donation came from the RE Corps Committee. However, these donations were not enough and the appeal was widened to firms and organisations, who had formed their own Auxiliary Bomb Disposal Units for their own protection, or who had benefited from the work of Bomb Disposal Squads RE in ridding them of UXB's from their premises. There was a most generous response, which enabled the Silver Centrepiece Committee to go ahead without financial restrictions in producing a centrepiece of the finest workmanship obtainable in Britain.

Marston Barrett, Jeweller and Silversmith of Lewes was commissioned to produce the centrepiece and it was made by Messrs C J Vander Ltd of Hatton Garden. They were responsible for the complete production, including silversmithing, chasing and engraving. The design was created by Reginald H Hill MSIA NRD, according to the committee's specifications. The figures were modelled by the sculptor, Thomas Bayley ARCA, and the two plates were hand engraved and carved by G T Friend OBE.

The base consists of Italian Verte Royale Marble. The hand made model is made completely of hall-marked solid silver (London). The piece depicts a correctly timbered excavation on the top of which is a 500kg German UXB. An officer is handling a clockstopper magnet, whilst a sapper listens for the ticking of a clockwork fuze. Around the pair are the batteries for the clockstopper magnet and the leads to these and the electrical stethoscope. Over the pair is a gyn and tackle of the pattern used during the war. The detail is authentic, the only artistic licence being in the placing of the soldier and clockstopper batteries so near the bomb. In reality they would have been at a distance and the bomb would have been at the bottom of the shaft.

One of the panels on the base depicts the steaming out of the main filling of a bomb, probably because the fuze could not be removed. In the background is a vertical Merryweather boiler which is feeding steam into the bomb through a spinner jet. The other illustrated panel show beach mine clearance in progress. One man uses the "Polish" mine detector whilst the others use an ERA mine locator.

The third panel carries the monogram of the Corps of Royal Engineers.

The above was copied from the official document which was issued at the time of the unveiling of the centrepiece in the Officers Mess of HQ BD Units (UK) in 1965.

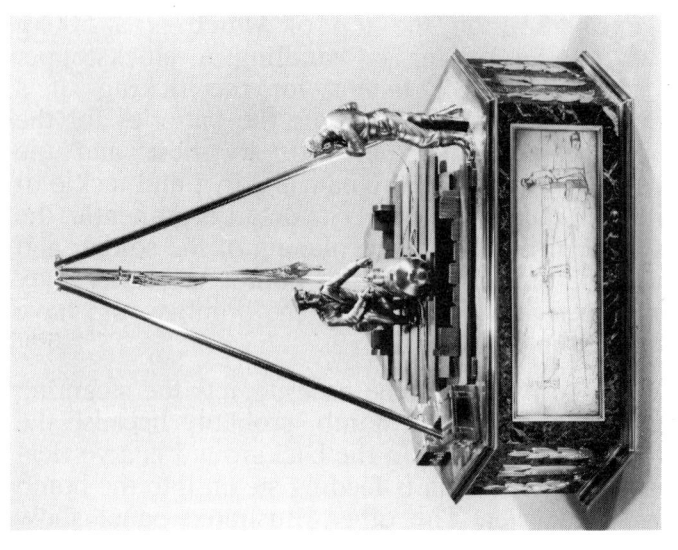

Two views of the Bomb Disposal Silver Centrepiece. Photos courtesy of Col B S T Archer GC OBE ERD.

244

Appendix 'G'

CONTRIBUTORS

My grateful thanks to all who contributed their stories and photographs upon which this book is based. All served in Royal Engineer Bomb Disposal Companies during the 1939/45 war, or in the years immediately after.

Capt D L Anderson

Col B S T Archer GC OBE ERD

Capt H W Beckingham

Sgt C E Brinton BEM

Sgt W Edwards

Spr G Fielding

Lt Col C H Green GM

Capt A F J Hannaford

Sgt O A Kent

Major J Melrose ERD

Sgt F G Norman

Major G R Ovens TD

Sgt E Rylance

Capt C V Sadler

Major J H Setchell MBE ERD

Lt Col P S Wadsworth

Capt C Walker

Major N P Woollven TD

Major H Yard ERD

My thanks, also, to the officers of EODTIC (Explosive Ordnance Disposal Technical Information Centre) for their assistance in providing historical information.

A special thanks to Mr Steve Venus, who has not served in B D, but is an Associate Member of the B D Branch of the Royal Engineers Association and a Researcher and Collector of mines, bombs and fuzes. He has been a great source of background information for this book.

Finally, my grateful thanks to Mrs S Brown, the daughter of Major W L Andrews GC, who made available her father's diary, his B D Course notes, photographs and newspaper cuttings.

Some of the information contained in this book was taken from the War Diaries of the B D Companies, which are held in the Public Record Office at Kew.

Index

PERSONNEL MENTIONED IN TEXT

248